The Novice Teacher Survival Guide

How to Avoid Personal Injury and Major Property Damage

Justin Case

**Dedicated to the laughter
that leads to introspection ...**

Copyright © 2021 by BilMor Studios, LLC

All Rights Reserved. No part of this publication may be reproduced, stored in a retrieval system, or transmitted in any form or by any means, electronic, mechanical, photocopying, recording, or otherwise, without prior written permission from the author.

Printed in the United States
ISBN: 978-0-578-76768-0

- - -

Cover Illustration: Ard Hoyt
Educational Consultant: Jamie Massey
Reviewers: Michael England, Ben Hare, Stephanie Noles
Copy Editor: Talena Keeler
Distribution Manager: Shirley Knott

Table of Contents

Introduction — p. 5

The Teaching Space
The Well-Managed Classroom — p. 7
Creating an Effective Environment — p. 11

Tools & Rules
Rules of Engagement — p. 15
Effective Teaching — p. 23
Teaching Strategies — p. 31

Curriculum
State Standards — p. 41
Creating a Curriculum — p. 45
Lesson Planning — p. 51

School Culture
Building School Culture — p. 61
Professional Learning Communities — p. 75
Response to Intervention — p. 83

Assessment
Formative Assessment — p. 89
High-Stakes Testing — p. 97
Testing Terminology — p. 107

Postface
On a Serious Note — p. 115

Index — p. 125

About the Author — p. 127

"In the field of education, there are times when humor is our best defense."

References

Please note: Except for the final chapter, all references in this book are completely bogus ... just like most of those that you used for your college and university term papers.

More information can be found at:
https://zapatopi.net/treeoctopus/

INTRODUCTION

ACCORDING to classroom management expert, Harry Wong, "The fact that you have a college degree in English does not make you a teacher, much less an English Teacher." This is absolutely true ... unless, of course, your region is experiencing a major teacher shortage or you live in Oklahoma.

In that case, desperate state legislatures will allow you to teach English with a degree in Animal Husbandry or Bowling Industry Management, as long as you're willing to spend the next few summers snoozing through more university coursework, and you can eventually pass something called a Praxis test.[1]

If you agree to these terms, then the state Education Department[2] will immediately issue you a "provisional license," which allows you to stock up on essential teaching tools at the campus bookstore ... like diet soft drinks and Snickers® bars.

No, I jest. A provisional license allows you to spend your days managing a room full of hormonal adolescents just like a real teacher, even though you haven't actually had

---

[1] *This involves driving a fully-loaded Prius in parabolic arcs through the university parking lot.*

[2] *Due to budget cuts, now just a guy named "Ed"*

any training yet. Of course, this isn't a problem because, as all legislatators know, everyone is already an expert on teaching because everyone at some time or another went to school.

But then comes your first day of classes, where you will quickly discover that you really, really need this book! And that's a win-win situation since I really, really need to sell two million copies to help pay for the extended therapy required from a life-long career in education.

So sit back, relax, and enjoy the last few minutes of sanity in your life before your teaching career begins.

Disclaimer

Please note that this book is for entertainment purposes only.[1] Except for the final chapter, many of the concepts presented herein are completely useless and most are actually counterproductive.[2]

Or as the sign on the vendor cart says, "If you choke to death on a hot dog, that is natural selection at work, and the management assumes no responsibility."

---

[1] *Or possibly for entertaining porpoises. Sea creatures have a very low threshold for humor.*
[2] *Not unlike a few outdated "teacher prep" programs*

Chapter 1: The Well-Managed Classroom

LET'S start with what educators refer to as the "teaching space."¹ Here are the four primary signs of a well-managed classroom:

SIGN #1:
STUDENTS ARE DEEPLY INVOLVED WITH THEIR WORK

For students attending middle school, this primarily involves texting, eye-rolling, and amateur cosmetology. However, occasionally student work may also include teacher-led instruction ... especially on the single day each spring when teacher-evaluations occur.

When this happens, do not panic. A classic cultural film, like "Napoleon Dynamite," will often suffice, as long as it is accompanied by a suitable viewing guide. ²

As an added bonus, the darkened room will obscure

---

[1] *At least beginning teachers. After the first few months, the descriptions become much more colorful.*

[2] *Often something with "Sparks" or "Cliffs" in the title*

any ongoing activities the administration might deem inappropriate (see next section).

SIGN #2
STUDENTS KNOW WHAT IS EXPECTED OF THEM

Most students know that arson, extreme vandalism, and ritual sacrifice are generally frowned upon.[1] They understand the importance of being prepared for class by bringing snacks, social media devices, and personal grooming tools.

Most students also know that assignments should always be submitted somewhat near the so-called "due date," and mass exodus is not allowed until the agreed-upon signal ... usually a bell, buzzer, or the shout, "Fight! Fight!"

SIGN #3
THERE IS LITTLE WASTED TIME, CONFUSION, OR DISRUPTION

Experienced teachers will tell you that focused student engagement is vital. Any other option can often be life-threatening.

Methodologies for achieving "time on task" range from keeping them distracted with a guest speaker (see "ritual sacrifice" above), to boring them into a stunned stupor with informative lectures. One good example would

---

[1] *Except in certain sections of inner-city New York*

be a detailed description of the difference between a pronominal adjective and an agrarian pangolin.

This last method carries the potential for constant re-cycling since (based on current brain research) the average student is incapable of remembering any portion of a presentation for more than 10 minutes.

SIGN #4
THE CLASSROOM CLIMATE IS PEACEFUL AND PLEASANT

This is easier to achieve than one might think. Simply wait until all the students have exited the building for the day, gather up any items that have been left behind,[1] and replace any upturned furniture.

This is also a good time to make notes on your lesson plans ... such as "never, ever attempt the Skittles activity again!" and "avoid approaching the proximity of any student who had gym last hour."

See, peaceful and pleasant.

---

[1] *Such as empty pizza boxes and flame throwers*

"While handcuffs and tear gas may be effective, their use is generally forbidden."

Chapter 2: Creating an Effective Environment

IN the last chapter, we discussed four signs of a **Well-Managed Classroom**. But that, of course, begs the question, "Now what's for lunch?"

It also begs the question, "What are the best ways to create an effective teaching environment?" Here are some specific tips from the experts [1] ...

TIP #1:
MAKE SURE THE CLASSROOM IS READY FOR YOUR STUDENTS

Teachers who prepare their classrooms in advance can minimize the potential for personal bodily harm. As far as possible, remove everything from the room which can be thrown, stolen, or set on fire.

Remember that bare walls may inspire creativity (usually in the form of graffiti [2]), so cover them colorful posters

---

[1] *Teachers who have survived for more than two years without incurring a permanent disability (scars do not count)*

[2] *The Italian word for "giraffe"*

containing inspirational thoughts such as, "Be the bridge and people will walk all over you," or "Whatever career you choose will soon be done by robots."

TIP #2:
WELCOME YOUR STUDENTS
AND MAKE SURE THEY KNOW
WHERE TO GO

Clearly describing the precise location of all restrooms in the building will help clarify this and minimize any unexpected unpleasantness.

TIP #3:
WHAT YOU DO ON THE FIRST DAY
OFTEN DETERMINES HOW MUCH RESPECT
YOU WILL RECEIVE FOR THE REST
OF THE SCHOOL YEAR

Because this is true, it's always a good plan to call in sick the first day. Better yet, claiming that you have contracted a highly contagious disease can help you miss the entire first week.

When you do return to class and students ask where you've been, be prepared with comforting answers like, "My parole wasn't complete until yesterday," or "I was the keynote speaker for the national Extreme Martial Arts conference."

To support these assertions, wearing a prison-issue orange jumpsuit or a karate-gi on the day you return may also prove helpful.

TIP #4:
ARRANGE STUDENT SEATING TO HELP MINIMIZE BEHAVIOR PROBLEMS

Assigning troublesome students to seats in another teacher's classroom is one useful strategy.

However, if your principal insists that your students remain in your room, try arranging their desks in geometric configurations. The resulting confusion will distract them for quite some time, especially if you change the patterns weekly.

Ability grouping is also popular since students who share common interests (like DIY explosive devices or witchcraft) will often keep one another engaged for an entire class period with minimal teacher interaction.

Under no circumstances should you place any student's desk next to yours. Like ebola patients, most students are best kept at a safe distance.

"Engagement in the classroom rarely involves impromptu marriage proposals."

Chapter 3: Basic "Rules of Engagement"

THIS chapter has some real meat in it![1] You'll discover the top ten ways[2] you can keep your students "actively engaged" (which is teacher-speak for minimizing the student snooze-cycle). We've got a lot of ground to cover, so buckle up!

RULE #1:
USE STRUCTURED MOVEMENT TO KEEP YOUR STUDENTS FOCUSED

Begin the class period by asking all of your students to stand beside their desks and join in a simple "Go Noodle®" activity. Although a few students will merely raise their eyebrows at this, most will break into hilarious laughter (while still sitting firmly in their chairs). This has the double benefit of encouraging students to stay put while also starting the day off on a lighter note.

A word of caution, however. If any of your students

---

[1] *Or as they say in school lunchrooms, a "meat-like substance"*
[2] *Actually only eight, but "top ten" has better alliteration*

watched the movies **Footloose**, **Stomp the Yard**, or **Feel the Beat** the previous evening, all bets are off!

RULE #2:
CREATE ACTIVITIES TO ENCOURAGE COLLABORATION

Divide your students into teams. Correction: *attempt* to divide your students into teams, then wait until (like a bargain-store granola bar), they fall into random clumps. Give each group a pair of scissors [1], a sheet of yellow construction paper, 15 spaghetti sticks, and a 12-inch strip of duct tape. Now have them construct a replica of the largest structure in your community. [2]

The resulting chaos is guaranteed to keep your students "engaged" long after the class period is over, the bell rings, or the riot police arrive.

RULE #3:
TAKE ADVANTAGE OF DIGITAL PRESENTATION SOFTWARE

Digital presentation software like PowerPoint®, Prezi®, and Keynote® provide exciting new ways for students to harass and annoy their classmates.

Of course, digital presentations can also be created by the teacher. This allows you to demostrate your ability to use thirty different "slide transition effects" within a

---

[1] *While shouting, "Danger Will Robinson! Danger!"*
[2] *Rural communities may substitute Bill O'Reilly or Rosie O'Donnell*

ten-minute presentation. New audio technology even allows these transitions to be enhanced with sound effects ranging from "thunderous semi-automatic weapons" to "projectile vomiting." While the end result may not be educationally valid, it will certainly be memorable.

RULE #4:
USE WRITING PROMPTS TO PROMOTE STUDENT REFLECTION

When interest in your digital presentations begins to fade [1], you can often reawaken student interest with an engaging "writing prompt." This is a short phrase, sentence, or even a picture that is intended to give students a focus for their writing. [2]

Traditional writing prompts [3] are often boring and outdated, so strive to use prompts that your students can easily relate to, such as:

"The most interesting thing about county lockup is ..."

"Ain't no one got no bef with Eminem 'cause ..."

"I been saving up for an awesome tattoo of ..."

"You can slurp spaghetti through your nose if you ..."

... and similar timely topics.

---

[1] *On average, five seconds after sound effects echoes die out*
[2] *Conceived by someone who's never actually seen a human child*
[3] *"What I did on my summer vacation that I'm willing to tell you about, no really, this actually happened!"*

However, at all costs avoid any writing prompts that might lead to critical or strategic thinking. If your students develop such higher-level skills, it might render them unfit for many employment opportunities such as port-a-pottie pumper, pet food taste-tester, or mascot for the local "Mr. Pickle" franchise.

RULE #5: TO AVOID DEAD TIME, OFFER CLEAR PRECISE INSTRUCTIONS

The term "dead time" is not really what it sounds like … at least not if you keep your guard up. It refers to those periods of time when you've lost student attention and nothing productive is taking place.[1]

To re-engage student attention, many teachers rely on various scripted routines such as "One, Two, Three. Eyes On Me," or the bi-lingual VASS system.[2] Auditory cues, like a simple chime or bell, can also be useful. These are often followed by the traditional screamed threats.

After allowing a couple of weeks to establish these routines, your students should be able to actively ignore you in a much more structured way. Always remember that complete and total student engagement is easily attainable in any training video that is filmed using professional child actors.

---

[1] *Essentially the period between September and June*

[2] *For **Ven Aquí! Siéntate! Silencio!** (Loosely translated: "Come here! Sit down! Shut Up!")*

RULE #6:
PERSONALIZE STUDENT LEARNING THROUGH DIFFERENTIATION

Differentiated Instruction helps engage all students by providing a wide range of avenues to learning. This allows your diverse community of learners[1] to approach challenging problems in their own unique way.

For example, take a typical math problem: "You have 23 artichokes. How do you divide these equally among your 6 friends?" Of course, the correct answer is, "You give each friend 3.83333333333333 artichokes." But diffentation allows each student to apply his/her own unique background and experiences to the equation, resulting in such stimulating responses as …

"I have six friends? Really?!"

"Put 'em in a blender and make soup out of 'em."

"Four. I bought another one so it would be easier."

"What the #$@&%*! is an arti-thing, and why would anyone want twenty-three of them?"

By allowing a variety of answers, you not only engage all students, but also ensure that they're better prepared to deal with future real life situations — such as helping wealthy strangers safely transfer millions of dollars from a Nigerian bank account into their personal account (current balance = $13.72) merely by providing their social security number and secret password.

[1] *a.k.a. Children of the Corn*

RULE #7:
EMPLOY A "MAGIC MUG" TO KEEP STUDENTS ON THEIR TOES

Your classroom should always be a place where students are encouraged to take risks without fear of ridicule.[1] Using the "Magic Mug" strategy will help ensure that no individual student feels picked on when it comes to answering questions.

Here's how the process works: First, write each student's name on a wooden Popsicle® stick. (To avoid the risk of rabies or the plague, use washed sticks from orange mango popsicles, which no one ever eats anyway.) Now place these sticks in a colorful coffee mug with an inspiring educational slogan.[2]

When it's time to answer questions, pull a stick from the mug at random and call on that student for a response. The terror this inspires will raise the level of student engagement to new heights. It can also be quite inspiring to hear the resulting gasps and moans, even if you're just reaching for a sip of coffee.

RULE #8:
USE MULTIPLE TEACHING STRATEGIES

Finally, a bit of variety can go a long way in increasing student engagement, so feel free to mix and match the most currently popular teaching strategies.

---

[1] *Ridicule should be reserved exclusively for clueless visiting legislators.*
[2] *"Teaching is as easy as riding a bike ... through an F5 tornado."*

Cooperative Learning: This strategy encourages students to work together in "teams" and to share their different points of view. Each member must actively contribute in order for the group to be successful. By grouping students with highly diverse interests,[1] you can have them at each other's throats in no time.

Inquiry-based Instruction: Here students are presented with an "essential question," then use their problem-solving skills to propose answers. While well-designed questions lead to deeper understanding of academic concepts, the use of highly-ambiguous questions results in a variety of unexpected and amusing outcomes.[2]

Learning Stations: These are classroom "centers" where students can complete the same task, but at a level and style specifically designed for them. Students change stations when signaled, so watch closely so you can interrupt whenever you note any kind of progress.

Remember, to be most effective, strategies should be changed every day (or even mid-class). If your students have no idea what's coming next, there's no time for them to prepare a reasonable line of defense, and so they must collaborate simply to survive.

---

[1] *Try "Power Lifters with Chess Club," or "Yuppies with Goth."*
[2] *"Hair-pulling, teeth gnashing, and the occasional tortured scream*

"A quieter classroom can often be achieved by substituting glue sticks for lip balm."

Chapter 4: Effective Teaching

EFFECTIVE teaching can greatly increase student engagement through clear, focused instruction. Here's a closer look at the characteristics shared by the most effective and engaging lessons.[1]

A CLEAR LEARNING OBJECTIVE

A "learning objective" is a clear, concise description of what will be learned and how it will be assessed.

While learning objectives often go by different names[2], the primary purpose is always to help your students focus on academic learning ... as opposed to devising clever ways to hang the teacher from suspended ceiling grids using only rubber bands and paper clips.

The lesson's learning objective must be appropriate to the grade level being taught, and should be clearly displayed in a prominent place.[3] This allows students to easily avoid eye contact with that part of the room when encouraged to recall the lesson's purpose.

---

[1] *Other than the practical kind you get by licking a frozen lamppost*

[2] *"Daily Lesson Target," "Purpose Statement," and "Pay Attention You Idiots!" are just a few*

[3] *Avoid using permanent marker on your forehead.*

Make sure that students clearly understand how their mastery of the learning will be demonstrated or assessed. For example, a lesson on fire safety might be assessed by randomly setting fire to a popular student, then seeing how long it takes for the other students to extinguish the flames.

No, I jest. Obviously this would be an unacceptable assessment since it is a group activity rather than an individualized test of student knowledge.

Be sure to refer back to the lesson's learning objective at strategic points thoughout the hour. This will help keep your students actively engaged as they look aimlessly around the room searching for the clearly posted objective until the bell rings.

AN ANTICIPATORY SET

The "anticipatory set" is a short introduction to the lesson that is designed to set the stage for learning. It often includes a "hook" to grab students' attention.[1]

Common methods for conducting an anticipatory set include explaining the purpose ("There will be a test on this!"), linking the lesson to prior learning ("We began talking about this yesterday, right before the bomb scare."), or previewing the learning ("The RPRGR-ESR is the ratio of product returns to gross revenue excluding sales receipts, which will be very useful if you're ever involved in falsifying tax returns.").

[1] *As in illegal fishing," the bigger the hook, the better!*

TEACHING IN CHUNKS

Like most adults, students have very short attention spans. By dividing each lesson into short chunks of five to seven minutes, you can force your students to spread their inattention over multiple opportunities for learning instead of just a single session each hour.

Begin each chunk by demonstrating a single brief step, procedure, or observation that is directly related to the lesson's learning objective.

Here's an example from a lesson on the importance of being prepared for class:

1) If you don't bring a pen or pencil to class, you'll have nothing to write with.

2) If you have nothing to write with, then you can't take any notes.

3) If you can't take any notes, then you can't study.

4) If you can't study, then you'll fail this class.

5) If you fail this class, then you won't graduate.

6) If you don't graduate, you probably won't get a job.

7) If you don't get a job, you won't have any money.

8) If you don't have any money, you won't have food.

9) If you don't have food, you'll be really, really skinny.

10) If you're really, really skinny, then you'll be ugly.

11) If you're really ugly, you won't get married.

12) If you don't get married, you won't have children.

13) If you don't have children, you'll be all alone.

14) If you're all alone, you'll be depressed.

15) If you're depressed, you'll can get very sick.

16) If you get very sick, you will die.

Therefore, if you don't bring a pen or pencil to class, YOU WILL DIE!

So as you can see, teaching in chunks allows you to show your students how each step in a process leads to an ultimate, logical conclusion.

GUIDED PRACTICE

Immediately after each chunk, give your students the opportunity to imitate or practice the learning that has just been taught.

For example, using the preceeding example, allow your students to immediately lose their pens, not take notes, and not study. They can then spend the rest of the hour looking forlornly at each other, and visualizing what they'll look like when they are old and lonely.

During this time, carefully observe your students as they practice their new skills to ensure that they have mastered the objective. However, be aware that reactions to this particular lesson can be misleading, since sorrowful faces and heavy sighs are common in teenagers, and not to be confused with mastery.

CHECKS FOR UNDERSTANDING

"Checks for Understanding" (CFUs) are simple, quick assessments of each small step. These can take place both during and after each Guided Practice.

Recent studies about the effectiveness of CFUs suggest that researchers can get paid for studying just about anything. But it's important to note that CFUs have been shown to not only increase student learning, but also to keep wearers afloat in the event of a water emergency (or is that Compact Floatation Units?).

Regardless, the most common methods for conducting CFUs include observing students as they work, [1] cold-calling on students randomly, [2] having students hold up whiteboards with the answer, [3] or using interactive technology such as Kahoot. [4]

Be sure to maintain the lesson pace by limiting any attempts to help individual students during this time. Individual tutoring should take place during the next chunk while other students are busy actively ignoring the assignment, making them much less likely to have time for creative activities behind your back. [5]

---

[1] *While the "deer in the headlights" look often indicates possible confusion, it may also simply indicate a case of constipation.*

[2] *Guaranteed to give students ulcers*

[3] *Ignore the signs that say, "I hate you!"*

[4] *A game-based learning platform, used in the few schools that can still afford educational technology*

[5] *Shooting spitwads, throwing machetes, or rappelling*

MONITOR AND ADJUST

Based on what you have observed during the CFUs, you can quickly adjust instruction as needed for each step. This often involves re-teaching the concept or clarifying your expectations.

Get your point across with simple, direct explanations such as, "You were supposed to write the answers on the worksheet, not carve them into your desk top," and "By 'demonstrate that you understand the basic mechanisms of pain and the structures involved,' I did not mean for you to stab your friend with a pencil."

You can also have students pair up to assist each other in understanding the concept presented.[1] When peers share new ideas in their own language, it often results in a quicker path to mastery. For example, here's a direct transcript of two students sharing ...

Student A: "Wha'du git fa number tree?"

Student B: "I think it was a verb or something."

Student A: "K ... tanks."

Be sure that the majority of students have mastered the concept before moving on to the next step. This helps them avoid missing key components of instruction such as what page the answer key is on, or the fact that tomorrow is an early dismissal day.

---

[1] *For grouping suggestions, see page 21.*

INDEPENDENT PRACTICE / ASSESSMENT

A good way to assess students' mastery of the material by asking them to complete a task that requires applying the concept taught in the preceeding chunk.

For example, if the focus was "verbs," simply have them use one correctly in a sentence ... such as "This sentence has a verb in it." This allows your students to successfully demonstrate that they have mastered the daily learning objective.

Ultimately, you want your students to progress from a point where you are providing all the instruction, to where they are functioning independently. In other words, they are doing the work, not you. [1] This process is often referred to as the "Gradual Release Model."

In addition, this is the correct time to provide small group instruction or individual tutoring to those who are still needing assistance. [2] By now, the rest of the class has probably fallen into a dazed stupor, so taking your eyes off them for a few moments drops the hazard level to roughly the equivalent to disarming live explosives. So enjoy this momentary lull in your day.

---

[1] *Which is only fair since you're getting paid less than that plumber who clears the school's stopped up drains every week*

[2] *That boy named Bryun [3] and two kids who don't speak English*

[3] *Whose parents were creative spellers, illiterate, or both*

"When instructional excellence fails, there's always intimidation."

Chapter 5: A Closer Look at Teaching Strategies

BACK in Chapter 3, we took a brief look at some common teaching strategies. In this chapter, we'll take a more detailed look at the major teaching strategies you learned about in college.[1]

DIRECT INSTRUCTION

Direct Instruction is a "teacher-directed" method where the instructor stands in front of the class, clearly presenting the information to be learned[2]. This method is also known as TBLA.[3] Advanced versions of TBLA may involve drawing charts, graphs, or cuneiforms on a whiteboard, or occasionally using a transparency placed on an overhead projector (which for some reason sits on a desk or table, rather than hanging above you as the name would imply).

Successfully using Direct Instruction requires that the teacher have the students' full attention at all times ...

---

[1] *Assuming you weren't complete distracted by pheromones*
[2] *Or slowly repeating, "Bueller? Bueller?" Bueller?*
[3] *TBLA = Terminally Boring Lecture Approach*

which is rarely possible, unless you somehow manage to spontaneously combust.

SCAFFOLDING

The goal of scaffolding is to move students progressively closer to a complete understanding of a particular concept or skill by providing successive levels of temporary support. Like a real scaffold, this allows your students to achieve heights they would be unable to reach on their own.[1]

As students progress, these temporary supports are slowly removed until without any additional assistance from the teacher, they are able to fail independently.

COOPERATIVE LEARNING

As stated in Chapter 3, Cooperative Learning is one of today's most popular strategies.[2]

This approach organizes the classroom into groups, maximizing opportunities for both academic and social learning. Researchers often refer to this as "structured positive interdependence."[3]

While Individualized Learning (page 34) can often be competitive in nature, Cooperative Learning requires students to work together, capitalizing on the unique

---

[1] *So they can hang toilet tissue from the gym rafters*
[2] *At least according to the authors of books on this topic*
[3] *A technical term for highly-complex interactive chaos*

resources and skills of each individual group member.[1]

Cooperative Learning activities include asking for information, evaluating one another's ideas, monitoring one another's work, and eventually engaging in active, aggressive intragroup combat.

Over time, the teacher's role in Cooperative Learning changes from actively presenting the lesson's concepts to quietly facilitating the learning process.[2] Typical Cooperative Learning tasks are often challenging, creative, open-ended, and intellectually demanding ... which is why this strategy is now in decline.

CONCEPT MAPPING

A "concept map" is a hierarchical diagram designed to illustrate the relationship between various topics or concepts. In other words, it's a bewildering bunch of circles or boxes connected by lines to other confusing circles or boxes. By using these two-dimensional graphic interfaces, you can expand your students' level of confusion exponentially.[3]

One form of Concept Map is the "flow chart," which is beloved by human resource departments everywhere. Since virtually every student you have is doomed to eventually become a "human resource," be sure they are familiar with this insidious tool.

[1] *Competitive speed eating, nocturnal lock picking, knife juggling, etc.*
[2] *i.e. - reading the most current fashion magazine*
[3] *Except for Bryun, who has already reached terminal confusion*

An educational Concept Map typically represents ideas and information through a series of interconnected circles, generally with the most important ideas at the top and the least important at the bottom. In their most virulent form, these maps may also include arrows and color-coding.

A frightening variation of the Concept Map is the so-called "Mind Map." This is a graphic representation of what is happening in a student's mind when he/she is processing a particular concept.[1] When given the topic, "repairing damaged relationships," for example, the typical teenage Mind Map (adjusted for gender accuracy) would look something like this:

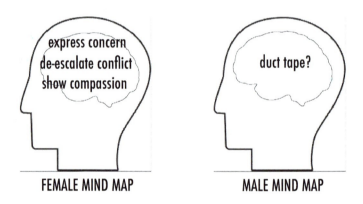

INDEPENDENT LEARNING

Independent Learning is when a student is able to think, act, and pursue their studies with only minimal support from a teacher. Obviously, this strategy is a myth.

[1] *Assuming, of course, that actual cognition is taking place*

INQUIRY-BASED INSTRUCTION

Inquiry-Based Instruction was developed during the "discovery learning" movement of the 1960s by educators who favored certain herbs that are illegal in most states except Colorado. It was a reaction to traditional forms of instruction [1], where students were required to memorize the capitals of European countries that no longer exist.

Speaking of Europe, in merry old England this strategy is referred to as "Enquiry-Based Instruction" ... which just goes to show that Brits can't spell.

Instead of presenting established facts, the teacher introduces each lesson by posing questions, problems, or scenarios ... such as "why is there a comma after the word 'problems' in this sentence?" [2] The students (who you should refer to as "inquirers" [3]), are then required to identify and research specific issues and questions that can help them on their journey to developing meaningful solutions ... or a migraine.

One common variation of Inquiry-Based Learning is "Problem-Based Learning." In this strategy, a group of troublesome students is locked away in an airless box and given 45 minutes to find their way out. The real-life similarities to the classroom are obvious.

---

[1] *See TBLA on page 31.*
[2] *Only Oxford comma fans will get this one.*
[3] *The subsequent looks of confusion are priceless.*

K-W-L

This rather awkward acronym[1] stands for what students already **K**now, what they **W**ant to know, and what they think they will ultimately **L**earn.

Here's how it works: When the teacher is ready to introduce a new topic, he/she asks the students to brainstorm everything they know about the topic. This allows them to fill the K column of the K-W-L chart with misinformation and random doodles.

Next the teacher asks the students to write down what they "want to know" about the topic. This results in the W column of the K-W-L chart remaining blank.

During and after reading the selection, students refer back to the K and W columns. When sufficient time has passed,[2] the teacher asks the students to write what they have learned in the L column of the K-W-L chart. The success of this last step often depends on whether or not the assignment will be graded, or whether or not an "A" student is sitting in close visual proximity.

LEARNING STATIONS

Learning Stations are a flexible grouping strategy that allows different students to complete the same task, but at a level and style that meet specific needs.[3]

---

[1] *Latin for "aggravating abbreviation"*
[2] *Or the teacher desperately needs a bathroom break*
[3] *Including the teacher's need to distract students like Bryun*

Students of all ages will benefit from the change of pace a Learning Station provides, and the expanded opportunity for creative expression. [1]

Learning Stations come in many varieties. Here are some of the most common ...

Communication Station: There are many forms of communication (reading, writing, speaking, listening), and this station allows students to experiment with all of them simultaneously. The resulting din can be heard several classrooms away, letting other teachers know that an "interactive activity" is underway.

Writing prompts [2] are a common Communication Station feature, as is a stack of high-interest books. [3] You can also encourage verbal communication by providing a simple recording device. Take time to listen to what your students have to say. This will allow you to learn much more about your students. [4]

Science Station: Sharp objects, slimy goo, and deadly insects are all inherently fascinating to children. Be sure you have a ready supply of each.

By allowing students to explore the excitement of scientific concepts through challenging experiments,

---

[1] *Fighting for supplies, hair pulling, screaming, etc.*
[2] *See page 17.*
[3] *The Poo Chronicles; Earwax for Everyone; Explosive Games; etc.*
[4] *"Last night when daddy was making mef, it blew up!"*

you can simultaneously promote experiential learning [1] while rapidly reducing class sizes. Science stations also offer cross-curricular opportunities in first aid, triage, CPR, and emergency response.

Math Station: This is one of the easiest stations to create. Simply gather a stack of worksheets and a small supply of calculators. Now add a group of students with black, heavy-framed glasses, button-down shirts, and pocket protectors.

Manipulatives, such as tanagrams,[2] are also useful. The truly creative student can rapidly turn these into deadly projectiles, adding an element of surprise and wonder to the classroom.

Art Station: (Please note that the term "art" is being used rather loosely here.) Start by stocking your Art station with markers, poster paint, glitter, watercolors, crayons, stickers, glue sticks, stray cats, and other simple materials. These can be easily combined to create a record-breaking disaster within minutes.

You will soon discover that your students' creativity will soar as they decorate not only the walls and floor of the classroom, but also each other. The results can often rival Piacasso at his finest, or the work of a street artist who expresses his genius by dumping cans of paint on random spectators.

[1] *Also known as "learn by doing" … or sometimes "learn by bleeding"*
[2] *Ancient Hebrew for "those triangle thingys"*

NON-LINGUISTIC REPRESENTATIONS

Often referred to as the "Forrest Gump" strategy,[1] NLR is based on the clever use of analogies. These are often represented as a string of oddly-punctuated phrases like "Fish:Tank::Chicken:_____."[2]

These "A is to B as X is to Y" analogies can be very useful in teaching. This is because it can take your students most of the class period to figure out what they're supposed to do with them, and then keep them busy for the rest of the week trying to come up with some kind of an answer.

For example, with the NLR above, your students will scramble to determine the appropriate relationship between a fish and a tank. This will result in a variety of diverse theories from guppies in steel containers to aquatic, quasi-military applications.

Once your students have finally analyzed the initial relationship, they still have to figure out part two. The more they attempt to do this, the more frustrated they will become ... until eventually, they fry the fish, puncture the tank, and eat the chicken.

---

[1] *Due to his famous quote, "life is like a something something"*
[2] *"Coop" ... although "Nuggets" is acceptable if you're hungry.*

"Common Core
has nothing to do with
sharing an apple."

Chapter 6: State Curriculum Standards

In the preceding chapters, you learned how to create an effective classroom environment and mastered multiple strategies for instruction. But what are you actually supposed to *teach*?

NOT THE COMMON CORE!

Unlike most countries, America does not have national curriculum standards. Instead, each of our 49 or 50 states[1] has it's own unique set of academic guidelines. This allows them to eliminate references to embarrasing little historical faux pas like Jim Crow laws and to promote more enlightened views like "Moses was the primary influence for the U.S. Constitution."[3]

The idea that a student educated in Houston might learn different "facts" than one educated in Portland raised concerns with a few busybodies.[4] And so they commissioned the creation of a set of basic expectations

---

[1] *Well-worn textbooks may not include Hawaii.*[2]

[2] *And if it's not in the textbook, it doesn't exist. Nalowale!*

[3] *Unfortunately, as Texas readers know, I'm not making this one up.*

[4] *Governors and Education Commissioners from 48 states*

for student performance ... a simple compilation of what students should know at each grade level in each subject area. These new standards would not mandate what teachers had to teach (curriculum) or how they had to teach it (instruction). *Individual schools* were to decide how best to meet the standards, and how to help their students develop the critical-thinking, problem-solving, and analytical skills needed to be successful.

And this evil elitist attempt to destroy the very souls of our children became known as **The Common Core**.[1]

But shortly after these new standards were introduced, they ran into the super-shredder of politics. Several states made them disappear faster than a fat man flying down a waterslide.[2] Legislatures immediately spent millions of dollars creating "more sensible" systems. Never mind that these new systems were strangely similar to the Common Core Standards (including an identical numbering system). These states proclaimed victory over evil and students were safe again!

Thus, depending on which state you teach in, your standards may be based on the Common Core, a re-branded and sanitized version of the same, or a hastily thrown together hodge-podge of old benchmarks, regional superstitions, and political biases. In other words, "standards" are no longer standard.

[1] *Cue ominous background thunder.*
[2] *Specifically my Uncle Henry, a definite scale-tipper who once achieved terminal velocity at Dollywood*

STANDARDS vs. CURRICULUM

As stated earlier, standards are simply learning goals for what students should know and be able to do at each grade level. Like the framework of a house, they provides a basic structure for a host of other things (siding, roof, plumbing, heat and air, etc.) that get tacked on to make a home.[1]

Continuing the analogy, these "other things" are the curriculum ... the academic content chosen by local schools that is then reflected in specific courses. Curriculum can also include detailed, day-to-day lesson plans for implementing that content.

Thus standards are broad outlines, and curriculum deals with specific content. See the difference? And that means that (Facebook memes to the contrary), there is no such thing as "Common Core Math."[2]

Okay, so maybe we got a bit too serious in this chapter. But then, you can always go back to watching those humorous cat videos on Facebook. Not only are they amusing, but they actually reflect more reality than the majority of Common Core memes.

---

[1] *In many southern states, this may include the hides of recently-deceased animals.*

[2] *You'll have to find something else to be outraged about.*

"Proper curriculum alignment often requires the skills of a licensed chiropractor."

Chapter 7: Creating Your Curriculum

In the last chapter, we discussed state curriculum standards, and how they form the framework for building an effective instructional program. But what should you do if you work in a state that expects you to create your entire curriculum from scratch?[1]

CREATING A CUSTOM CURRICULUM

Here are the five key steps in creating your very own custom curriculum:[2]

Describe your vision. If it's 20/20, you're home free. If you wear glasses, fake it.

Identify your resources. Unless you bought them yourself, there aren't any. Most modern classrooms start out as bare as a depression-era pantry. Teaching is the only occupation where people steal office supplies from home to take to work.

---

[1] *Short of returning to your old job at McDonalds, which may not be possible due to that "exploding Big Mac" incident*

[2] *Which will be obsolete after the next election, regardless of the winning party since politicians thrive on change*[3]

[3] *Or large denomination bills if they can't snag change*

Identify Student Needs. According to researchers,[1] basic student needs include a safe environment, a sense of belonging, a feeling of competence, the need for active enjoyment, and freedom of expression.

A "safe environment" may be obtained by careful implementation of individual cubicles of bullet-proof glass. A "sense of belonging" and a "feeling of competence" are often gained through gang-related activities involving extortion and grand theft. The need for active enjoyment is a bit more difficult since killer dodgeball[2] has been banned. However, extreme skateboarding and decorative acupuncture may provide reasonable alternatives.

But freedom of expression? Well, this is *school* after all!

Develop Your Objectives.[3] A "learning objective" is the expected goal of a unit or lesson with regard to the demonstrable skills or knowledge acquired by the student as a result of the instruction. Posting open-ended phrases like ...

"Today we will —,"

"So we can —," and

"We've achieved mastery when —"

... is a great way to help you and your students focus on the lesson's stated objective.

[1] *Political jargon for "I'm making this up"*
[2] *Once the aphrodisiac of sadistic coaches everywhere*
[3] *Other than "survival" ... that one is a given*

Here's an example: "Today we will mix bleach with various household chemicals." "So we can see what happens." "We've achieved mastery when at least half of the class passes out." Ah, success!

Create Instructional Units to Meet Objectives. This step is so significant that we've devoted the entire next section to explaining it.[1]

THE INSTRUCTIONAL UNIT

While reflecting on the steps in the previous section, use your state's curriculum standards (see Chapter 6) as a framework to start crafting daily lessons. The more engaging your lessons are, the more you will keep your students' attention riveted.[2]

Begin by planning "instructional units." An instruction unit is a set period of time, ranging from a week or two to an era or an eon, that is organized around a central theme or topic such as "ancient torture systems" or "the dangers of bovine flatulence."

It's important that each instructional unit include a variety of textual materials, hands-on experiences, demonstrated skills, and meaningful assessments. This will allow your students to master a wide repertoire of competences and content ... or more importantly, appear to be fully awake during any unexpected classroom monitoring.

[1] *It was that or pay full price for two seats in coach.*
[2] *If this doesn't work, feel free to use actual rivets.*

To assess the quality of your instructional units, ask yourself the following four questions: [1]

Question 1: Have I aligned this unit with the state's curriculum standards, the district's guidelines, and my stated objectives? In other words, do I have any earthly idea what I'm trying to achieve here (other than convincing the principal that my IQ is higher than the cafeteria's carrot casserole)?

Let's suppose that the state standard is, *"Describe the universe. Give three examples."* To meet this standard, asking your students to inflate a vinyl blow-up model of the Earth is woefully insufficient. They will need to inflate at least three. [2]

Question 2: Does this unit contain a sufficient supply of teaching strategies, learning strategies, investment strategies, dating strategies, and gourmet coffee? [3]

Question 3: Does this unit offer authentic tasks that will engage a diverse group of learners? By diverse, I mean whatever groupings are the least offensive to the greatest number of people. [4] (Although in some settings, diversity might simply mean one or two students who think the principal's jokes are actually funny.)

---

[1] *Answering yourself aloud is discouraged. People tend to stare.*
[2] *The other 8 or 15 planets don't matter ... nor do areostars, galaxies, or other vintage Ford products.*
[3] *To keep you awake while students struggle with the rest*
[4] *Categories like sex, ethnicity, and income-level just seem to get people all stirred up ... especially sex.*

Question 4: Are the unit's formative and summative assessment opportunities designed to clearly measure the knowledge and skills that were overtly identified in the previously stated objectives?

Frankly, I have no idea what that last sentence even means, so let's wind this up.

CURRICULUM MAPS

The process described in this chapter is sometimes referred to as a creating a "curriculum map." And like a vintage road map, a curriculum map is designed to unfold in unexpected directions, totally blocking your view out the front windshield.[1]

So if you carefully followed the steps in this chapter, you now have a splitting headache. You should also have a curriculum map composed of properly-aligned instructional units. This will help you securely navigate from one meaningless point to another.

In the next chapter, we'll examine the individual components that make up an instructional unit. These are known as "lesson plans."

---

[1] *That 20 car pile-up in Poughkeepsie was not my fault.*[2]
[2] *No really, it wasn't! I use Siri.*[3]
[3] *The difference between Siri and an annoying spouse is that when Siri says, "Turn left, you idiot! LEFT!", you can throw Siri out the window.*[4]
[4] *This is not generally recommended with spouses.*

"No plan ever survives initial contact with the enemy."[1]

---

[1] *This is a quote from the famous Prussian military commander Helmuth van Moltke. While classroom teachers are not normally ruthless, blood-thirsty warriors,*[2] *there are still marked similarities in the job descriptions.*

[2] *With the possible exception of Mr. Hinklemyer, my 10th grade Algebra teacher*

Chapter 8: Tips for Effective Lesson Plans

Even though you wrote those three practice lesson plans during your teacher training ... well, the fact is that you're still going to be ill prepared for the tsunami of planning that will bury you during your first year as a classroom teacher. But never fear! The Justin Case method of intensive instruction will take you from amateur to expert in just a few short pages. [1]

ESSENTIAL QUESTIONS

Curriculum experts [2] insist that every good lesson begins with an "essential question." So let's begin with some essential questions about lesson planning.

Students: *"What are the social, physical, personal, and emotional needs of my students?"* Actually, this is an area you really don't want to delve into, especially if you are a high school teacher. (Remember what your "needs" were in high school?) It's also probably illegal to ask.

Strategies: *"Which teaching strategies will best enhance my students' learning?"* We spent a lot of time carefully

---

[1] *Without even the phrase, "But wait, there's more!"*
[2] *People who make a living writing books, not teaching*

reviewing the most common teaching strategies back in Chapter 5. Weren't you paying attention? No? Then drop and give me ten!

Grouping: *"Should I group my students heterogeneously or homogeneously?"* This is a problematic question, especially if you have difficulty with multi-syllabic words. [1] So like a good teacher, I'll help you break it down.

First "heterogeneous." Hetero is the Greek god of noisy flatulence. [2] Geneous means … er, generous. So in order to group your students hetergeneously, you would simply divide them up according to their degree of offensive smell. Thus you would place the boys who just came in from gym class in one group, place a mix of moderately clean students in the second group, and allow that tiny cluster of prissy girls holding their noses to form a third group. See how logical and easy that is?

Now on to "homogeneous." We've already established that geneous means generous (as in "a lot"), so we only need to add the homo. [3] Contrary to what you may have heard in sixth grade, homo simply means "the same." So homogeneous means "a lot of the same." Thus a homogeneous grouping would be … er, would be … a lot of … uh, the same you see. Not as simple as a heterogeneous grouping, of course, but it does serve to emphasize the importance of understanding Greek and Latin roots. [4]

[1] *Any words longer than "beer" or "brats"*
[2] *Also known as "Farticus"*
[3] *Cue snickers from those gym class boys*
[4] *Which can be quite tasty in Mediterranean cooking*

Timing: *"When is the best time to present this lesson? And are there prerequisites that my students must master before we begin?"* The importance of prerequisites is often overlooked. Obviously you cannot begin an intensive discussion on the proper use of square roots until your students have mastered the nuances of epic poetry. This would be ludicrous. [1]

Regarding "when," the ideal time to present any lesson is immediately after lunch. This is because the majority of your students will be slumped over in a nearly unconscious stupor. (Cast-iron corndogs and toxic tater tots can be your friends.)

Materials: *"What sort of materials do I need to supply for this lesson?"* First, never write a lesson plan that involves the use of Skittles® or M&Ms®. These innocent, colorful manipulatives can instantly become vicious tripping hazards or perilous projectiles! In addition, students are perpetually hungry, so there's a good chance your lesson plan will suddenly disappear.

Second, materials of a noxious or explosive nature should be limited to Home Ec class. [2] However, in this era of Top Ramen® and frozen pizza, those courses no longer exist. A suitable substitute might be a child-care class (diapers are notoriously noxious), a Freshman biology lab (where explosions are common), or any other venue with delicate and fragile surroundings.

---

[1] *Heterogeneous' first cousin*
[2] *Many believe "Ec" is short for Economics. But "Ec!" is actually a common response to food once produced in these settings.*

Outcomes: *"Was this lesson successful?"* If none of your students appeared to slip into a coma, then give yourself one point. If at least two of your students appeared vaguely interested, give yourself five points. And if one of your students appeared to actually learn something,[1] give yourself a full ten points.

This is also a good time to ask yourself, *"What would I do differently next time?"* Common answers include "eliminate pounding on the lectern," "use more effective visuals,"[2] and "choose another career."

Sequence: *How can I improve my instructional pacing?* Smoothly flowing lessons will help keep your students focused. Purposeful pacing lets you effortlessly transition from one section of the lecture to the next. This allows students to gauge how close they are to accomplishing the lesson goal, and well as judging how soon they can stampede back into the hallway.[3]

Rationale: *What was my primary reason for presenting this lesson?* Can you say "paycheck"? Ha ha. Actually thinking about your rationale provides a framework for future planning. It's forces you to reflect on why you used a particular book, video, or teaching strategy. For example, "I know Susie hates Chaucer, but she was only marginally annoyed ... so next time I'll use Beowolf!"

---

[1] *Other than today's lunch menu*

[2] *Replace charts and graphs with live reptiles*

[3] *The school hallway is a unique ecosystem designed to allow growing children the maximum opportunity for Darwinian interaction as they wander from one tribal region to another.*

DAILY LESSON PLANS

With answers to the essential questions firmly in mind, we can now move on to compiling specific activities and content that you are supposed to teach. This is known as a "daily lesson plan." Good daily lesson plans usually contain the following five components.

Lesson Objective: As we discussed in Chapter 7, objectives are the expected goals of the instruction ... the skills or knowledge that will be demonstrated by the student as a result of his/her interaction with the content (in spite of your lame presentation skills).

Objectives should always be clearly defined and must contain enough detail that a substitute teacher could use them to cover the material should an emergency[1] prevent you from being at school.

Delivery Method: There are numerous methods for delivering content to your students. Always choose the one that will be the most effective for your specific audience. For example, dressing up as a major character from a beloved book will delight first graders, but the hookah-smoking caterpillar from Alice in Wonderland may not elicit the same reaction from high school students.[2]

Today, many schools use Chromebooks to assist with content delivery. This allows teachers to present the material without any direct human interaction ...

---

[1] *Like the one-day clearance sale at Kohl's*
[2] *Regardless of how much you assure them it's only herbal shisha*

much like a hotel lobby vending machine. And like this capricious candy conveyor, the lack of direct human contact can lead the user to shake, bang, and kick the device in a vain attempt to achieve results. (For those with an even greater aversion to student contact, UPS, FedEx, and USPS can be helpful tools.[1])

Materials Needed: Some lessons will require various supportive props (also knows as manipulatives, visual aids, or necessary distractions). Movable tiles, tangrams, and flash cards[3] are good examples. Like your can of pepper spray, be sure you have these close at hand so they are ready when needed.

Student Groups: Many experts believe that placing students in structured groups enhances learning.[4] Ability grouping (discussed in Chapter 2) is one popular way to group students. Other methods include peer-tutoring groups, cooperative groups, and jig-saw groups.[5]

One caution. If your lesson involves grouping students, be prepared for a moderate amount of disruption (i.e. - total chaos). Students tend to form tribal societies, and do not take kindly to anything which disrupts their primal interactions or attempts to redefine existing boundaries. So you probably ought to skip that whole hetero- homo- genie thing mentioned earlier.

[1] *Assuming you know your students' addresses* [2]
[2] *Which is probably a FERPA violation*
[3] *Flash cards do not involve trenchcoats.*
[4] *Some people also believe the earth is flat.*
[5] *This last method requires cooperation from the shop teacher.*

Assessment Method: A wide variety of methods exist to help you determine the effectiveness of your lesson. Often referred to as "formative assessment," this allows you to conduct in-process evaluations of student progress during and/or immediately after instruction.[1] Common formative assessments include ...

1) The Quiz - This traditional approach originated in ancient times with the Greek philosopher Biliousness.[2] Giving a quiz is somewhat easier these days since students no longer have to chisel their answers on rocks.

2) Response Cards - In this method, students simultaneously hold up white boards, magnetic boards, surf boards, school boards, and similar devices to indicate their response to a specific question or problem. This allows the teacher to easily note which students have eaten their markers.

3) Hand Signals - Early versions of this method had students show anywhere from one to five fingers to signal their level of understanding. However, due to student creativity in the use of *which* finger, more recent versions rely on thumbs up, sideways, or down.

4) Four Corners - The teacher makes a statement, then students indicate their response by moving to a designated corner of the classroom.[3] Corner choices might include "I strongly agree," "I strongly disagree," "Is this

---

[1] *Depending on how much coffee you consumed that morning*
[2] *Or was it Nauseous? Those ancient Greeks all look alike.*
[3] *Which may take some time if your class meets in the rotunda*

really going to be on the test?," and "I just want to stand next to Sheila."

> Note that this method combines progress monitoring with movement-based activity, which researchers say actively stimulates students' brains.[1]

5) Exit Ticket - End the lesson with a prompt which students respond to by writing on an index card. The teacher collects these "tickets" as students exit the classroom. Once all the students have left, the teacher then carefully deposits these in the trash.

6) Think-Pair-Share - This strategy gives students a few moments to think about a final question. They then pair up with a partner to argue about the answer before sharing their anger and frustration with the entire class. By starting with a sufficiently ambigous question, you can generate vigorous, intense debate.[2]

7) Reflection - During the final five minutes of class, have the students quietly reflect on what they've learned in this lesson. Dimming the lights and playing soft, relaxing music should quickly lull most of them into a nearly comatose state.[3]

However, be advised that to rouse them afterwards, you may have supplement the class-change bell by switching the music to AC/DC's "Back in Black."

[1] *Again, researchers will say almost anything.*
[2] *World War III*
[3] *Nebraska*

OTHER CONSIDERATIONS

Principals are sneaky buggers, and may want to check your lesson plans from time to time. Some principals even make a point of viewing plans weekly in order to provide input based on their own experience.[1] Be sure to find out what format is preferred since handwritten notes on the back of an envelope may not suffice.

If you don't use a pre-packaged electronic lesson planner (extremely simple, effective, and inexpensive ... and thus rarely provided by schools), consider creating a template of your planning page. Write in the activities that repeat each week,[2] then make several copies. Now just fill in the blanks on the copies with specifics for each week. As an extra precaution, do this in "doctor's script" so the principal has no idea what you've written.

Finally, be sure to complete your lesson plans well in advance.[3] This will help the lesson proceed smoothly ... at least until you're interrupted by a surprise assembly where an aging guest speaker dressed up as Tommy the Toothbrush will lecture about oral hygiene.

---

[1] *Often expressed through sports metaphors*
[2] *Take roll, scream at Tommy to sit down, etc.*
[3] *At least 10 minutes before class begins*

"One way to change school culture is to start wearing lederhosen."[1]

---

[1] *German for "funny looking britches"*

Chapter 9: Building a Positive School Culture

Let's begin by defining what we mean by "school culture." School culture is the environment that surrounds you each day. It's composed of the underlying attitudes, influences, and occasional odors that reflect your primary stakeholders'[1] beliefs.

This is also referred to as "school climate" ... but we'll ignore that term since it can be confusing, especially if someone else is controlling the thermostat.

TOXIC OR POSITIVE?

A toxic school culture may include students with little or no direction, teachers who have lost their purpose, an administration that is unreasonably demanding (or completely clueless), and a refrigerator in the break room that hasn't been cleaned in so long that it may contain emerging life forms.

In other words, it's the ideal environment for the opening scene of a movie where the new principal walks around holding a baseball bat.[2]

---

[1] *Stakeholder" = colleagues or students, not the cook at Outback*
[2] *Which seems strange since they never show a baseball team*

By contrast, a positive school culture results in a place where everyone's efforts are appreciated and all feel welcomed and loved. A place where people are informed and inspired through the power of unparalleled storytelling and creativity, and innovative technology leads to … oops, wait a minute. That's the mission statement for Disneyland. And since I can't afford the entry fee for all of you, we'd better move along.

Here are the top ten [1] proven ways to build a more positive school culture …

Create Positive Parental Involvement. Clear, open communication with students' parents can help avoid misunderstandings and remove feelings of mistrust or hostility. At least some of the time. Or maybe not. Sharing details about the cafeteria food fight episode or the accidental standardized test shredding incident might actually increase hostility.

But back to involvement. To increase your parent's role in school culture, start by asking them about their hopes and dreams for their child. [2] You can also plan special workshops where teachers and parents discuss homework, study skills, and tests. (Be sure to offer hazard pay for teachers willing to host such events.)

There are other ways you can involve parents in your school, too. Many parents will willingly serve on event

---

[1] *Definitely ten this time … unless one wanders off and gets lost*
[2] *Usually that their teen might leave home before he's thirty*

planning committees (to make sure their child is featured prominently), participate in school fundraisers (to make sure their child's extravagant uniform is paid for), or even help staff the concession stand at ball games (to make sure their child gets free hot dogs).

Celebrate Student Achievement. Publicly acknowledging student accomplishments can go a long way towards improving school culture. In addition to the traditional honor roll (which historically recognizes overachievers or kids whose parents write all their term papers), look for other ways your students can strut their stuff. Here are a few real life [1] examples:

- Last summer, Stan Still showed his amazing athletic ability by climbing the highest mountain in Florida.

- Shirley Knott exhibited her exceptional journalistic expertise by getting every teacher off-topic at least twice a week for an entire semester.

- Hunter Keye's emerging musical talents were finally recognized after a startling solo on his wind driven, manually operated, pitch approximator. [2]

Surprising talents like these often go unnoticed. But focused public recognition will cause other students to immulate the spirit of these accomplishments ... perhaps even breaking the Guinness World Record for anchovy consumption or nose typing.

[1] *For a given value of "real" (think "reality" TV)*
[2] *Also known as a trombone*

And speaking of student achievement, don't forget to start a ritual tradition of ceremonial school awards! Your annual "Miss Tuna Fish Sandwich" trophy or "Extreme Ironing" endurance medal may soon be just as coveted as that traditional birthday sombrero in the Mexican restaurant of your choice.

Establish Values-based Rules. Rules are very important, but all too often they are stated in a negative fashion. However, you can create lasting values by focusing on positive statements instead. You can also combine several individual rules into a single generic irritation.

For example, instead of specific rules about chewing gum, water bottle usage, disruptive electronic devices, or flagrant flatulence, create a general school rule stating: "Don't be a dork." Note that when school rules are sufficiently ambiguous, it not only challenges students' thinking, but also cuts down on disciplinary reports since most teachers will have no idea whether or not a rule has actually been broken.

Promote Creative Discipline. Of course, when rules are broken, discipline must follow. But simply by broadening the acceptable range of responses, you can markedly change your school culture.

Let's say a student has stolen the coach's hidden stash of Copenhagen. After-school detention would be the traditional, boring response. However, making the student swallow the entire contents in less than sixty seconds will not only provide an entertaining interlude for his/her fellow classmates, but also offer the potential for cross-curricular applications. Future nursing students can practice basic emetic procedures. Future custodians can learn how to clean up unexpected messes. And future artists can attempt to determine the exact shade of green displayed in the resulting skin tones. [1]

By the way, let us not forget that in the 1700s, public hangings were a recreational opportunity attended by the entire family. While this may not be an acceptable form of discipline in your local community,[2] the basic concept of communal retribution appears to be alive and well with certain segments of our population (per several popular Facebook memes).

Model Positive Behavior. Most teachers have a mental list of specific qualities they wish their students would demonstrate. Some even display motivational posters around the classroom in the forlorn hope that these might not only be read, but also change behavior. (This is similar to the concept that if you gaze at thin people long enough, you will lose weight.)

But researchers tell us that the best way to impact student behavior is to *model* the conduct you would like to see. For example, sit quietly at your desk reading an inspiring book[3] for most of the class period. While you

---

[1] *Before implementing, please review the definition of satire.*
[2] *Unless you live in Alabama or Idaho*
[3] *Like this one*

may not actually impact student behavior, you will at least get caught up on your reading.

Encourage Social-Emotional Learning. School is not just about learning academic knowledge. Your students are also developing the social skills they will need to become competent, caring adults someday.[1]

Psychologists refer to this process as "social-emotional learning." To assist this process, you should offer helpful reminders throughout the day to encourage students in developing proper attitudes and behavior. Here are some typical examples ...

For the bully: "Please do not give Johnny a 'swirly' in the toilet again. That's not a good look for him." You can also use this as an opportunity to point the student towards a career in cosmetology where he can make good money creating horrible hairstyles.

For the cheater: "Cutting and pasting an entire page from Wikipedia does not meet the requirements for your end-of-course book report." To discourage such behavior, avoid any reference to how developing plagiarism skills might someday lead to adult career opportunities writing speeches for politicians.

For the practical joker:[2] "Replacing the chocolate chips in the cafeteria cookies with Ex-lax® was unacceptable.

---

[1] *Hopefully before retirement; after that it's probably too late*
[2] *See footnote #1 on previous page*

Next time, please use Prozac® or Paxil®." A deeper understanding of pharmaceutical substances and their properties may someday be an important skill in this student's adult life.[1]

By the way, it's important to note that helping your students develop such qualities as empathy, reliability, respect, and concern is vital ... especially since some of them may end up as future employees in the nursing home you will eventually occupy.

Create Rituals and Traditions. We touched on this earlier while discussing student achievement awards (and sombreros), but there are many creative ways to create new traditions. Consider these suggestions ...

R (our) Day: Start the year by telling your students that you will provide free donuts on the first day of every month that begins with R.[2] As an alternative, you can celebrate National "Talk Like a Pirate" day since "arrrr" is a pirate's favorite letter ... except for "c" (sea).

Tape the Principal Day: The original version of this event encouraged students to record witty sayings, aphorisms, and words of wisdom from the school's most prominent administrative leader.

However, in most schools this phrase now refers to a fundraiser where students pay a dollar each to purchase

---

[1] *Whether as a consumer or some version of Breaking Bad*
[2] *Spelling October backwards does not count.*

long strips of duct-tape which they subsequently use to mob the principal and stick him to the wall of the gym. This exciting tradition encourages school spirit and is great fun for everyone ... except perhaps the principal.[1]

Fish Festival Day: While similar events have always been popular in some regions, you can give your local school festival a unique twist by focusing the menu on invasive species. This not only adds an interesting environmental component, but even the preparations themselves provide an element of excitement.

For example, Asian carp are notorious for jumping out of the water when frightened. This can be extremely exciting when flying along in a bass boat at forty miles an hour. (Bam!) Or if you live in an Atlantic coastal community, catching a batch of lionfish can be equally intense. The sting from a lionfish can cause *you* to jump around even more than those Asian carp.

Career Day: Although "Career Day" has been around in one form or another for decades, today's changing societal norms have led to some interesting situations.

One kindergarten class in a southern state was enjoying a presentation from a student's father who worked in drug enforcement. A classmate, clearly not understanding, but wanting desperately to contribute, said "Then you prob'ly know my daddy. He makes mef."[2]

---

[1] *Especially when the teachers forget to take him back down*
[2] *The officer didn't, but made dad's acquaintance shortly thereafter*

Note that when inviting guest speakers for career day, some occupations you may want to avoid include dog food taste tester, professional sleeper, pole dancer, and drying paint watcher.[1]

Remember, creating new traditions with events such as these gives your students specific scheduled opportunities to be spontaneous, and they will definitely impact your school culture.

Inspire Innovation. Teachers are often encouraged to try innovative strategies in an effort to change their school's culture. Here are some possibilities:

Game-Based Learning: Free digital learning games are extremely popular, especially with teachers who forgot to write lesson plans. In one popular program, students must solve three math problems correctly, then can shoot aliens[2] for the rest of the class period.

Numerous studies have shown that digital learning games heighten levels of enjoyment and relieve stress. And besides this benefit for teachers, the students may occasionally learn something, too.

Media-Inspired Methods: The television and film industry provides another easily-accessible source of inpiration for new learning strategies. This has been especially true since the advent of reality TV.

---

[1] *As well as the occasional "Cuidacarro" from Costa Rica*
[2] *Aliens from outer space ... unfortunately, that's a necessary clarification these days*

For example, in order to increase your students' competitive drive, simply divide your classroom into teams, have them remove most of their clothes and paint themselves blue or red, and remind them that the losers will ultimately be banished to permanent locker room cleanup duty.

Note that if you choose to use The Hunger Games as your inspiration, you are sure to generate a lot of free publicity … not to mention an extended all-expenses paid vacation to county lockup.

"Less is More" Scheduling: One innovation gaining in popularity is the four-day school week. The claim is that having students attend school one day less each week can save up to 20% of the school's budget.[1] It's also claimed that this makes the profession much more attractive due to endless three-day weekends.[2]

One major downside is that free/reduced lunch kids will probably begin eating their textbooks on Mondays because they haven't had a decent meal in three days.

Promote Professional Development. Schools also impact school culture by providing opportunities for teachers to expand their instructional abilities and develop new skills through professional development. Based on decades of observing student behavior, some practical PD opportunities include:

---

[1] *Fact check: Research indicates average savings of less than 2%.*
[2] *So you can get a second job to support your teaching habit*

Student Swap Meet. This innovative pre-school event allows teachers to exchange students, increasing the effectiveness of classroom instruction. Conversations often go something like this: "I'll take Barney the Beast if you'll take both Wendy the Whiner and Spitwad Sam!" Like a competition poker game, stakes can be high.

The Technology Inservice. When conducted by experienced Information Technology professionals, this type of workshop can help better prepare you for interacting with students who are new to this country.[1] Be prepared for helpful hints such as: "In order to access student records, you simply need to apply the malleable logarithmic so that the two main amulites are in a direct line with the panametric data points."

Special Forces Recon. This type of training is especially popular in certain inner-city school districts. The ability to instantly blend in with your surroundings in a covert manner is not only an essential survival skill, but can also help you secretly monitor some of your students' unofficial, more notorious activities.[2]

As a corollary, an effective school leader should always solicit feedback on what teachers think and feel, not only about professional development, but also about school policies and new state education laws. Note that this works best in electronic form since written responses might require a flame-proof box.

[1] *Since neither group uses English as their native language*
[2] *Like collecting counterfeit Pokemon cards*

Improve the Physical Environment. Not surprisingly, physical surroundings can have a marked impact on school culture. The more comfortable your classroom, the more likely your students are to quickly drift into a drooling comatose coma (since most stayed up all night playing *Carmageddon Extreme*).

One recent study found that outdated classroom furniture can lead to a 36.7 percent decrease in student learning. Surprisingly, this same study determined that the problem can be completely eliminated by purchasing a special body-molding chair for each student at a cost of only $699.99 each. [1]

Other studies have shown that factors like light, temperature, and air can significantly impact the learning process. So be sure that your classsroom is equipped with all of those.

More recently, there has been a focus on classroom wall colors. Preliminary results indicate that different shades have strikingly different effects. Blue seems to be soothing and calming, red tends to encourage excessive excitement, and the ever popular government greenish-brown almost always induces nausea.

Some researchers even suggest that overall student learning can be increased by contrasting three neutral walls with one bold accent wall. [2]

---

[1] *The first study to include a 10% discount coupon on the back*
[2] *Including a giant graphic of the word Ole'!*

Regardless, making your classroom the most pleasant environment possible is always a good investment ... at least until the students arrive.

PATIENCE PAYS OFF

Remember, building a positive school culture takes a lot of time and effort, and there will be many hurtles and other sports-related analogies along the way.

But with great dedication, hard work, and constant reminders that "beatings will continue until morale improves!" you can achieve your goal before the school year ends ... and then start all over again next fall.

"The key ingredients for a PLC are peanut butter, lettuce, and chutney."[1]

[1] *Feel free to create your own tasty PLC combinations like **Papaya, Linguini,** and **Celeriac.***

Chapter 10: Professional Learning Communities

Despite what you may have heard, the acronym PLC does not stand for Post-Lunch Coma.[1] Instead, these letters refer to the "Professional Learning Community" - an ongoing process in which educators work collaboratively[2] in regularly repeating cycles to discuss data about student progress.

To be truly effective, each PLC meeting must be have a clearly-defined goal. Often that goal is to determine why the grade immediately below yours keeps sending you such poorly-prepared students. Unless, of course, you are a Kindergarten teacher. In that case, you know that the problem is the parents.

FOUR ESSENTIAL QUESTIONS

In order to achieve a sustained focus on learning, every PLC must address at least one of four questions:

1) What do we want our students to learn?

2) How will we know if they have learned it?

---

[1] *Unless you succumbed to those corn dogs and tater tots*
[2] *Teacher-speak for "argue"*

3) What do we do with students who haven't learned it?

4) What time do we break for lunch?

For a deeper understanding of PLCs, let's look at each of these questions in detail …

Question 1:
"What do we want students to learn?"

Naturally, the correct answer is "the state standards." (Give yourself two points.) But as we already know from Chapter 6, that answer is ambiguous at best. So here's the Justin Case compilation of the most essential skills that students need to learn …

First, students must to be able to read fluently and efficiently. Without this key skill, they have no way of interpreting the charges on the arrest report.

Second, they must be able to write clearly and coherently. Close attention to this subject in school can help students avoid "writer's block"—which is when a large square object[1] appears on your desk preventing you from writing.

Third, they must demonstrate an undestanding of basic math. This can be helpful when shopping department store clearance racks, or attempting to change price stickers on luxury items at the grocery store.

---

[1] *In college, these square objects often contain pizza.*

Fourth, they must be able to apply basic science principles. The ability to drive a 15-year-old minivan with bad brakes through the mall parking lot while avoiding vehicular manslaughter is a good example.

Fifth, they must understand essential concepts from social studies. This is handy when they become parents and have to set up international boundaries throughout the home to keep siblings from engaging in global thermonuclear war.

Finally, as the liberal arts crowd constantly reminds us, they should develop skills in art and music. In later years, this will allow them to snobbishly roll their eyes at any art or music that was created more than two years past their high school graduation date.

What all of this really boils down to is the expectation that after five or six years of high school, your students can enter the world fully-equipped to take on common "adult tasks" — like sitting up late at night to write an essay for their child's English class.[1]

Question 2:
"How will we know they learned it?"

A later chapter in this book (Formative Assessment) will deal with this question in great detail, since trying to determine exactly what has lodged in your students' brains is only slightly less complicated than charting

---

[1] *Tip: Avoid words like "henceforth". Those are a dead give-a-way.*

the Brownian motion of interactive teenage relationships. Suffice it to say that we will explain many useful technical testing terms such as "formative," "summative," and "thermonuclear."

Question 3:
"What do we do when they haven't learned it?

First, avoid the temptation to blame the underlying causes (bad parenting, extreme poverty, inbreeding, etc.) While this is often entirely accurate, it will win you no friends, and may even get you shot. [1]

Instead, keep your focus directly on the instructional process itself. Here are three simple questions that will help you zero in on areas for future improvement:

1) Did you use the most effective instructional strategy for presenting the lesson? There are plenty of strategies to choose from. For example, think-pair-share is a popular method where the student gives a piece of oddly-shaped fruit to a friend.

2) Were your students sufficiently engaged with the material? Were they clearly absorbing the content? [2]
If your students wander aimlessly around the classroom (or out the door) during your presentations, you many want to take a closer look at this one. Duct-taping them to their chairs only goes so far.

---

[1] *Especially south of the Mason/Dixon line*
[2] *Eating pages out of the textbook does not count.*

3) Do your lessons include "real world" examples that students can relate to? Instead of counting gold stars, try counting live cockroaches. An essay about "my summer vacation" could be replaced by "my six weeks in juvie." And instead of focusing on invisible bacteria, explore the wonderful world of actively-growing mold.

The act of reflecting about instructional processes can help you determine exactly what changes are needed in order for more students to master key concepts ... or it may just give you a headache. Either way, you've accomplished something.

Question 4:
"What do we do when they already know it?"

Previously, I referred to this question as "When do we break for lunch?" I'm sure you realized this was a joke ... because few teachers actually *get* a lunch! [1]

Be that as it may, in many districts this is a question that you'll never need to address. What minimal background knowledge students may have possessed upon entering school has been sucked out of their brains by social media and copious consumption of Red Bull®.

But if you do need to deal with those "gifted and talented" students [2], here are some tips that may help you maintain at least a portion of your self-esteem:

---

[1] *At least not in any recognizable form*
[2] *Anyone who plagiarizes less than 50% of the time*

1) Keep in mind that regardless of appearances, you are smarter than they are.[1] Nod a lot and try to say as little as possible in their presence in order to avoid disspelling the illusion of your superiority.

2) Gifted students are often geeks, so your extensive knowledge of fantasy/sci-fi movies can be quite useful. Endless arguments about plots and sub-plots, depth of villiany, time travel, and similar minutia can consume several class periods with lively discussion.

3) Gifted students often demonstrate an advanced ability to manipulate and play with words. Be prepared for paronomasiac comments like, "Coffee has a rough time. It gets mugged every morning!" While painful, such remarks are usually not fatal.

THE FORGOTTEN QUESTION

Some educators believe that Question 4 leads to a 5th question that often gets left out. PLC teams collaborate to carefully select essential standards. They identify the assessments that will help determine if students have learned those standards. They create focused interventions to support students who are not yet proficient.

... and then they run out of time.

---

[1] *Always post your framed degree in a prominent location.*[2]
[2] *Unless it's from a "for-profit" institution with a name like* **Washington Lincoln Jefferson Yes-Really University.** *Then the less said, the better.*

So the 5th question becomes "How do we find the time to effectively address Question 4?" Unfortunately, that's beyond the scope of this book.[1]

THE ULTIMATE GOAL

In summary, making sure that each PLC focuses on the four essential questions will help you and your colleagues maintain a sustained focus on learning to recite the four essential questions.

This ability will not only impress any members of the state department of education who happen to drop by, but will also prove that you do indeed know how to count to four.

---

[1] *Author-speak for "I don't have any good suggestions and there's no room for it in this chapter anyway."*

RTI should not be confused with RHCP[1] **... although both begin with the letter R.**[2]

---

[1] *Red Hot Chili Peppers ... an American rock band known best for living under a bridge*

[2] *A letter that is also quite popular with pirates*

Chapter 11: RTI - Response to Intervention

Response to Intervention (RTI) is a planned, multi-tiered approach to the early identification and support of students with learning and/or behavioral needs, as well as students who are exceptionally gifted.

Properly implemented, RTI can create a comprehensive cultural shift in your school that can increase student achievement while reducing behavioral problems. [1]

MULTI-TIERED SUPPORT SYSTEM

In some states, RTI is known as MTSS (Multi-Tiered Support System). This is, of course, a much better description of what the system is and what it does ... which is why the term is not used universally.

KEY COMPONENTS

Successful RTI is based on four key components:

High Quality Instruction: The foundation of RTI is high-quality, evidence-based instruction in all general education classrooms. This vital component should comprise

---

[1] *The theory is that students who are actually learning have less time for creative distractions like arson and assault.*

at least 80% of your RTI program.

Please note that "high-quality" does not refer to your students' mental state due to the consumption of questionable substances ... and "evidence-based" has no reference to the number of times each week that law enforcement visits your school.

And while high-quality instruction does indeed exist, in many regions, it is as rare as integrity in a politician. (So it might be a good idea to reread Chapter 4.)

Adequate Screening: Universal screening takes place in Kindergarten, 1st, and 2nd grades. Select screening (based on need) takes place in all other grades.

This is especially important if you live in a region where mosquitos and other flying pests are common. Adequate screening will prevent their entry into the classroom and the subsequent disruption of learning by swarms of blood-sucking creatures.[1]

Three Tiers of Instruction: The core of RTI is based on three-tiers of progressively intense instruction.

1) **Tier I** is all about core instruction. This is the foundation upon which the rest of the program is built. And if the foundation is not sound (like that d@*#! discount concrete you let your brother-in-law talk you into), one

---

[1] *Not to be confused with state evaluation teams, which can be equally disruptive.*

rainy night your lakeside cabin will slide down the hill into said lake, resulting in multiple lawsuits, a permanent family feud, and ... well, the less said the better.[1]

2) **Tier II is for students who need "supplemental" instruction in order to succeed.** This is often conducted in small groups or one-on-one with a trained Interventionist. Perhaps the student's reading or math skills are not quite up to par. Perhaps they need extra time to master basic science concepts. Or perhaps their teacher simply doesn't get Simpson's style humor and desperately needs a break.

3) **Tier III is for those students who need "intense, personalized" instruction.** This is always one-on-one and involves regular, structured interventions that address basic concepts like reading comprehension, math skills, and not setting fire to the teacher. And for some odd reason, the primary focus is usually those subjects that are featured in high-stakes tests. (See Chapter 13.)

Since some teachers gain a deeper understanding of complex topics through a visual representation (they don't like to read), the "RTI Pyramid" was created.

Here is one version of this graphic model (next page) that clearly shows the relationship between the three Tiers of instruction. This simplified version can be used to make individual teacher decisions.

---

[1] *This is, of course, just an analogy. Any resemblance to actual persons or actual events is purely coincidental ... right, Charlie?!*

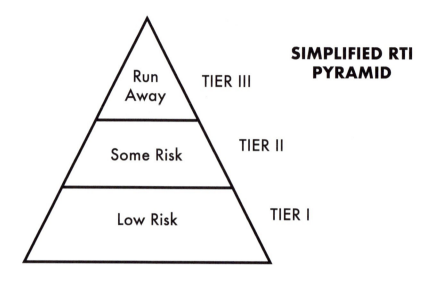

SIMPLIFIED RTI PYRAMID

Progress Monitoring: Most importantly, there must be continuous monitoring of individual student progress using Data.[1] Without adequate monitoring, it is impossible to determine a student's current status and whether or not he/she moved to Montana three weeks ago.

RTI TEAMS

Creating specialized teams is often the best way to implement RTI. These teams meet regularly to assess student data, to propose solutions (where growth does not meet expectations), and to consume copious quantities of heavily-caffeinated beverages.

Data Teams: Data Teams focus on overall systemic needs, not individual students. This can happen at both the building and district level. Data Teams give administrators a reputable source of information that they'll

---

[1] *If Data is unavailable, another Star Trek character may be substituted. (Except Worf. Klingons are not suitable monitors.)*

need when blaming Intervention Teams for lack of student progress.

Intervention Teams: Intervention Teams focus on the needs of individual students. They use data to determine progress, and spend long hours reviewing chart, grafts, spreadsheets, and creative granola recipes. One major qualification for membership is the ability to employ intense eye-rolling and deep sighs.

RTI - A FINAL ANALOGY

In business, you hear a lot about ROI (Return on Investment). Companies are constantly evaluating the amount of effort needed to generate better profits. In many cases, a moderate amount of focused effort up front can yield enormous benefits down the road.

So think of RTI as ROI for schools. A modest amount of effort up front can definitely end up sending you down the road ... to the nearest location where you can purchase an adult beverage.

"Formative assessments are tests used to test if students are prepared for the test that determines whether they are ready for testing."

Chapter 12: Formative Assessment

Formative assessments include a wide range of formal and informal tests that teachers conduct during the learning process. (The dreaded "Friday quiz" is a good example.) Experienced teachers know that the primary purpose of formative assessment is to give your students something to keep them busy while you update your Facebook posts.[1]

No, I jest. Formative assessments are actually designed to help you modify your instruction to improve student learning. For example, if you give a test and a high percentage of your students fail, you should consider re-teaching the material in a way promotes student interest and involvement.[2]

Of course, making the lesson more engaging and relevant is fairly simple if the only teaching you did on the first round was to assign a chapter in the text and tell students to do the even-numbered questions at the end. Watching paint dry is probably more exciting (and informative) than that traditional approach.

[1] *Or you watch humorous cat videos on YouTube*
[2] *Like using humorous cat videos in all future presentations*

But have no fear! Here are six Justin Case "formative assessment strategies" that almost anyone [1] can use.

One-Minute Papers: The "one-minute paper" is usually done at the end of the day, and takes less than an hour to complete. The teacher writes the focus question on the board,[3] then students attempt to write a sixty-second response summarizing what they have learned. Typical questions and answers include ...

Q: *"What was the main point of this story?"*
A: Well this guy was mad at this other guy because the guy before that told him that this other guy had done that thing that the first guy was mad about.

Q: *"What surprised you most as you were reading?"*
A: Erik jabbing me in the butt with his pen.

Q: *"What questions were not answered by this story?"*
A: Whether Maria is going to go out with me.

Q: *"What was most confusing about this topic?"*
A: What topic?

Without this type of formative assessment, you might never know that your students haven't mastered the material until they fail a quiz or test. But by regularly using the one-minute paper strategy, you ultimately will

[1] *As long as they're teachers, not shark fishermen or pole dancers* [2]
[2] *Ethic performers from central Europe*
[3] *Or for the tech savvy, displays the question on the screen*

have fewer students failing your tests because they're skipping school and won't be there to take them.

3-2-1 Countdown: This is a variation on the "end-of-day" formative assessment. Start by giving your students index cards to write on.[1] Now have them respond to the three following questions ...[2]

1) What are three things you didn't know before?

2) What are two things that surprised you?

3) What is one thing you want to start doing because of what you have learned?

Proponents of this method say the response to this last question is a true test of the relevance and meaning of the lesson. This is because humans always want to apply what they've learned in some way.[3]

Think-Pair-Share: This simple strategy was discussed briefly in the last chapter. Here's how this method is supposed to work ...

1) The teacher asks the students a question.

2) Students write down their answers.

3) Students then turn to their partner and explain their response.

[1] *And giving a pencil to Bryun because he ate his*
[2] *To minimize inappropriate responses, steal their pencils.*
[3] *Which explains why bawdy limericks are so popular*

Theoretically, this allows the teacher to move around the classroom listening to various discussions, and thus gaining valuable insights into diverse levels of student understanding.

In reality, it works more like this ...

1) The teacher asks the students a question.

2) Some students momentarily look up from texting to determine if this activity will be graded, then return to categorizing their classmates.[1] The rest demonstrate the meaning of the phrase, "deer in the headlights."

3) When asked to pair up and share responses, most students enthusiastically turn to their best friend and immediately begin discussing plans for the weekend. The socially inept merely look around in abject terror.

Meanwhile, rather than move around the classroom gathering data,[3] the teacher returns to the relative safety of his/her desk and waits for the bell to ring.

Round Robin Charts: Contrary to popular opinion, this strategy does not involve obese birds. The process goes like this ...

1) Students are divided into small groups of three or four. Based on the various peer groups (see footnote),

---

[1] *Stoners, geeks, jocks, freaks, goths, skinheads, sluts, and wiggers*[2]
[2] *Don't ask.*
[2] *Always an "iffy" proposition*

this can take up to half the class period.

2) Each group is given a large sheet of poster board and some colorful markers. By the time you have finished handing these out and are ready to begin instructions, group one has already created a politically-incorrect protest poster which starts a fight with group two.

3) Once that issue has been resolved and the school resource officer has left your classroom,[1] have each group respond to an open-ended question with a single sentence or drawing. Remind them to leave room for the other groups' contributions.[2]

4) After a few minutes, have each group pass their poster to the next group ... who then writes their own sentence or adds their own drawing. Continue until all the groups have had a chance to participate.

Now share the combined knowledge of the class by hanging the posters around the classroom. Students will quickly point out their own work while totally ignoring the "lame" contributions of others.

Twitter Summaries: Twitter is a social media platform dedicated to the idea that human interactions are so shallow that they only require 140 characters to express a complete thought or begin a major controversy. Some teachers have brought this concept into the classroom

---

[1] *Regretting restrictions on the use of lethal force*
[2] *A tiny box in one corner with the caption, "make it fit, losers!"*

by having students write 140 character summaries in response to a question or topic of the day. The thinking was that this would force students into different modes of thought and require great attention to detail.[1]

It's important to note that in 2017, Twitter doubled the number of characters to 280. (Some believe this was because 140 characters were insufficient to make major policy statements or start global thermonuclear war.)

Extension Projects: Students can create projects to show their mastery of the concepts and skills you have been teaching. Even if these projects aren't complicated, they can help students demonstrate their ability to do higher-order thinking. Here are some samples of simple projects students can do ...

1) *Design an original piece of artwork that illustrates the subject matter.* This will bring out excitement and creativity in your students.[2]

2) *Record a podcast where a student panel discusses the topic.* This activity gives students an opportunity to imitate the type of professional dialog seen on major talk shows ... like screaming, name-calling, and the infamous angry pout.

3) *Build a model that represents the key concept behind the lesson.* For example, if the lesson was about ancient

---

[1] *These teachers had obviously never read an actual Twitter post.*
[2] *Extreme caution is advised if the subject was human anatomy.*

Rome, students can build a model of the Coliseum [1] complete with real human blood.

4) *Create an engaging PowerPoint®, Prezi®, or Keynote® presentation that features main points from the lesson.* As mentioned earlier in this book, [2] digital presentation software provides interesting new ways for students to harass and annoy their classmates.

SUMMARY

Now that you are armed with these clever and useful formative assessment strategies, you are prepared to wage war upon the uninformed and illiterate masses ... or your students, whichever are closest.

---

[1] *Technically the Flavian Amphitheatre, but who cares?*
[2] *See Chapter 3, Rule 3.*

"The term 'high stakes' has nothing to do with cannabis-consuming cows."

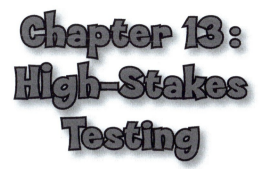
Chapter 13: High-Stakes Testing

Edward Thorndike (1914) once famously said, "If something exists, it exists in some amount; and if it exists in some amount, it can be measured." The attempt to apply this concept to characteristics like honesty, compassion, and love may explain why educational psychologists are often single.

This tendency to reduce everything to a set of numbers, combined with the "failing schools myth" (more on that later) has led to our modern obsession with high-stakes [1] testing. The theory is that an annual assessment of student skills will yield reliable information about the effectiveness of both teachers and schools.

In actual practice, this is similar to determining the quality of a couple's relationship by looking at a single snapshot taken during a high-stress moment. [2]

TEST RATIONALE

In addition, years of research have shown us that to accurately evaluate any kind of academic performance

---

[1] *Unpalatable even with A1 sauce*
[2] *Like when they're filling out their annual tax forms*

(student, teacher, or school), multiple data points are required. This is just common sense.

So when legislators in states across the country decided to create an "accountability" system to evaluate schools, natuarally they mandated a *single* data point system.

To make things even more interesting, several states now compile these the annual test scores into a "school grade." Like many legislative solutions, this is simple, direct, easy-to-understand, and completely meaningless.

But on a positive note, it does give your local constituency something else to get upset about.

TEST DESIGN

Testing companies are constantly assuring us that all test questions are thoroughly vetted by teams of nuclear scientists and nobel prize-winners. This is to ensure that their tests are "Valid and Reliable." [1]

Although many people still question the value of high-stakes tests, [2] there are several benefits to this prevalent form of child abuse. Here are a few ...

High-Stakes Tests Encourage Creativity. The completely mind-numbing nature of filling in bubbles encourages many students to form creative patterns with the answers, such as Christmas trees, battleships, and hearts.

[1] *"Valid and Reliable" - the advertising slogan for the Yugo*
[2] *Unless they make their living from the testing business*

Since this is more difficult with new computer-based tests, many students now "just choose c," or rely on a repetitive pattern like "a, then b, then c, repeat." [1]

High-Stakes Tests Measure Meaningful Skills. Multiple choice questions are a great way to evaluate the most important skills we want our children to learn ... except for little things like "creativity, critical thinking, resilience, motivation, persistence, curiosity, endurance, reliability, enthusiasm, empathy, self-awareness, self-discipline, leadership, civic-mindedness, courage, compassion, resourcefulness, sense of beauty, sense of wonder, honesty, and integrity." [2]

However, if you desperately want your child to be able to parrot back the definition of a pronominal adjective, these tests have got you covered!

Of course, high-stakes tests don't only contain multiple choice questions. They also offer a selection of "open ended responses." The answers students give to these questions are primarily graded by temps with no teacher training who make an average of $11 an hour. [3]

And since productivity is important, these graders must grade a set number of answers every hour. With such a carefully designed approach to qualitative evaluation, we can only assume their accuracy rate is quite high.

---

[1] *Unfortunately, this is actually true and not uncommon.*
[2] *See Gerald Bracey's "A Short Guide to Standardized Testing." Phi Delta Kappa Fastbacks 2000:7-52.*
[3] *Also actually true. (Besides, it beats flipping burgers.)*

High-Stakes Tests Mimic Real Life. We all know adult life can be enormously stressful, so this type of testing can give students a little taste of what lies ahead. The stress of high-stakes tests can create extreme anxiety in even the brightest of students. They can also make young children vomit or cry or both. Fortunately, teacher test training includes instructions on what to do when a student vomits on the test.[1]

High-stakes tests also help students understand the kind of pressure that encourages people to cheat or lie. And they can help prepare students for a life of competent mediocrity. Who could possibly want more?

TEST QUESTION EXAMPLE

Thinking back to my own testing days, I remember the excitement of being faced with questions that challenged by ability to extrapolate ambiguous facts and formulas. Many of them looked something like this ...

> 13. At what distance would an object obiting the Earth have a period of 100 min if mg = 4.57 x 10^{13}?
>
> a) The mid-point between Jupiter and Reno.
>
> b) Objects don't have periods, only sentences.
>
> c) What's magnesium (mg) got to do with it?
>
> d) All or none of the above.

Just imagine how useful knowing this kind of obscure

---

[1] *Again, this is actually true.*

information will be in encouraging your students and furthering their future careers.

FAILING SCHOOLS

At this point, it's important to note that the driving force behind high-stakes testing in our country is that America's schools are failing ... and failing badly!

According to most politicians (and testing companies), our schools have been failing for thousands of years, and this is entirely due to the poor educational policies of (insert name of opposing political party here).[1]

In fact, America's schools have been failing for so long that you can no longer expect rational behavior of any kind from anyone under the age of 50![2]

Of course, it doesn't really matter that the "failing schools" narrative is subject to interpretation[3]. Like any popular meme, if you repeat something often enough, soon everyone will believe it. (They couldn't post it on Facebook if it wasn't true, right?)

So here's an interesting fact: Even though Americans educate *all* our children (not just the elite), in 2016 America students surpassed Canada, Germany, and even Denmark in math and science on the internationally-recognized TIMSS test.

---

[1] *Or if you're really feeling nasty, specific congressmen*

[2] *Trust me on this one.*

[3] *i.e. - a total lie*

But to be fair, that was the week of the infamous Kim Kardasian/Taylor Swift feud, so no one in America really noticed. [1]

Besides, whether it's Madison Avenue or Washington, you should never let actual *facts* get in the way of a good narrative ... especially when it serves your purpose. And when it comes to selectively using information, advertisers and politicians do more "cherry-picking" than a California migrant worker.

BEHIND THE SCENES

Testing in America is definitely big business, and the rapid rise in high-stakes testing has been a huge boon to the industry. One of the largest testing companies in American now generates well over a billion dollars a year, and has a multi-acre corporate headquarters that rivals most Ivy League universities.

In addition, this company's CEO reportedly made in excess of 1.3 million dollars in 2016 (not counting an additional $42,000 in bonuses), and those numbers continue to rise. [2]

Of course, this clearly shows that the testing companies' only interest is in providing what's best for our nation's schools and for our children.

---

[1] *Trends in International Mathematics and Science Study ... and yes, these test results are actually true, too. Look it up!*

[2] *Not too shabby for a "non-profit" organization*

But like Don Quixote tilting at windmills, there are still some misguided educators who continue to challenge the wisdom of this massive, entrenched system. They're concerned about minor issues like these: [1]

1) **Significant scoring errors**. Obviously a somewhat overblown concern. Yes, there *was* that incident a few years ago where Hawaii had to replace one test publisher with another due to massive errors and distribution problems. But the second major testing company did much better. They only had one *small* glitch — the need to re-grade over 98,000 tests after students received scores for submitting blank test booklets.

2) **Lost instruction time.** It can't be that much, can it? Actually, most schools report allocating almost 25% of the year's instruction to test prep. Of course, the bright side is that the simplistic testing approach of choosing only "right or wrong" answers can help prepare your students for membership in any number of cults.

3) **Significant damage to children.** So what if a child has to repeat a grade or his/her high-school diploma is withheld based solely on the state test score? [2]

Well, as testing companies quickly point out, "we're not responsible for how our tests are used," and "no system is perfect; there are always unintended consequences."

[1] *This list is based on actual, documentable occurrences.*
[2] *As of this writing, there are thirteen states that use high-stakes test results as exit criteria.*

A LOGICAL SOLUTION

Numerous research studies have shown that there is a direct correlation between high-stakes test scores and a schools' socio-economic status. In other words, rich kids almost always do significantly better on standardized tests than poor kids.

In fact, if you create a graph of a state's school test scores and overlay it with a graph of their schools' free-reduced lunch status, the two are almost identical.[1]

Which brings us to the most logical solution ... **simply eliminate standard tests entirely and base a school's annual grade solely on their poverty rate.**

Think of it! States would save millions of dollars each year. Schools would save countless classroom hours spent preparing for state tests. Teachers and students would be saved from the anguish of dealing with "test day." Best of all, this new system would be every bit as fair and equitable as the current system.

Of course, there is a downside. Due to lost revenue, the testing czars would eventually have to vacate their palatial digs and seek more honest and productive employment. But as they so eloquently have pointed out, "no system is perfect, and there are always unintended consequences."

---

[1] *Once again, this is sadly true. (See NAEP data.)*

IN CONCLUSION

Some forms of standardized testing can be very useful and informative if properly applied.

However, like a junk-food junkie in a Twinkie® factory, legislators seem unable to keep their hands off the final product. Thus what *should* be simply one of several ways to evaluate student learning invariably morphs into a high-stakes test.

And to paraphrase Mark Twain, "That's the difference between the lightning and a lightning bug!"

"Data is a character on Star Trek who has an ultimate storage capacity of eight hundred quadrillion bits."[1]

---

[1] *This definition of "data" is from Wikipedia, and therefore it cannot reasonably be questioned.*

Chapter 14: Testing Terminology

So let's start with one of the basics. What is the difference between "criterion-referenced" and "norm-referenced" tests?

Criterion-referenced tests were first developed in the ancient kingdom of Criteria as a torture device for unruly children. A disgraced student was required to write the Criterian alphabet on the wall[1] fifty times, using a piece of chalk held tightly in his teeth. During this process, the student was constantly monitored by a trained observer (refereeus-officius), who could be easily identified by his black and white striped shirt.

Today, *criterion-referenced* refers to an attempt to measure whether an examince can display a clearly defined set of behaviors[2] that reflect an established unit of measurement. (Grade level equivalency is a good example. Johnny takes a test, and his score shows that his reading level is equivalent to that of the classroom's pet snail.)

By contrast, *norm referenced* tests are designed to determine an examinee's status in relationship to the

---

[1] *Smart boards had not been invented yet.*
[2] *Developed by social scientists, a.k.a. "so-so scientists"*

average score of a group ... more specifically, to how well guys named Norm performed. This is given in terms of a percentage, i.e. "Johnny scored in the 9th percentile" (which doesn't actually matter due to Johnny's consistant ability to score in the 9th inning).

BASIC TESTING VOCABULARY

Testing companies often use very specific vocabulary in their questions. This is because they have determined that if a student doesn't know what the term means, then he/she has little chance of arriving at the correct answer ... which allows them to make those graceful, flowing bell curves when charting test scores.

But clever teachers quickly realize that mastering the terms that testing companies use can greatly increase their students' success on standardized tests (thereby increasing their income in states with merit pay). Soon covert lists began to circulate as teachers wearing trenchcoats began to loiter on street corners looking to sell their findings to other desperate educators.

But fear not! The Justin Case "tantalizing table of testing terms" is just a short paragraph away! Free of charge, here are the top ten[1] terms that testing companies randomly insert into key sentences. (For ease of use, each term is defined, then followed by an example.)

Analyze: To break apart and explain how each part fits into the whole. "It was unnecessary for the prosecutor to

[1] *Actually eleven ... but again, "top ten" sounds better*

analyze how the mobster disassembled Mr. Jones since the victim's subsequent relocation to the inside of several suitcases precluded any chance of reassembly."

Argue: To defend one side of an issue using facts, opinions, etc. "To *argue* the point, Mrs. Smith stood behind the podium, bravely holding the angry students at bay by pelting them with etceteras."

Compare: To show how things are similar. "The class was asked to *compare* algebraic equations to medieval torture devices, noting common similarities."

Contrast: To show how things are different. "Describe the *contrast* between the meals served in a typical school cafeteria and actual food consumed in the real world."

Demonstrate: To provide a step-by-step procedure showing how to do something. "The students dove for cover as Mr. Fuentes attempted to *demonstrate* a basic chemical reaction by casually dumping an entire carton of Mentos® into a gallon of Coke®."

Formulate: To devise or to develop. "Michael worked hard to *devise* another formula for making himself attractive to cheerleaders once his accordian-playing approach proved ineffective."

Evaluate: To judge the worth or value of something. "It is difficult to accurately *evaluate* the worth of dissimilar substances like air and water, with the possible exception of when you are drowning."

Infer: To read between the lines.[1] "Due to the smoke curling out of his ears and the fact that his coat was on fire, the principal was able to *infer* that Bryun[2] had been attempting to secretly vape in the bathroom again."

Predict: To infer what will happen next. "The coach was able to clearly *predict* his future employment status when his team scored yet another goal in the wrong end zone."

Explain: To clarify by telling how something occurred. "Well this guy was mad at this other guy because the guy before that told him that this other guy had done that thing that the first guy was mad about."

Summarize: To express in as few words as possible. "Yeah, that."

ADVANCED TESTING VOCABULARY

Of course, should you decide to expand your career by attentding graduate school, you'll need to learn a more advanced set of testing terms. For example:

Accountability: Responsibility for educational outcomes, often measured through standardized testing. (Note that said accountability only applies to teachers, not to the legislators who invented the idea.)

Authenticity: A measure of how well a test reflects real-life situations. (In other words, not at all.)

---

[1] *Impossible for the literal-minded since there is nothing there*
[2] *That clueless kid from Chapter 4 whose parents couldn't spell*

Construct Validity: A computation of how well a test actually measures what it is supposed to measure. (See Authenticity.) Not to be confused with the thrash metal extreme band of the same name.

Cut-Off Score: The minimum score that a student must receive in order to be allowed to live. In certain southern states, this is also a measurement of the attractiveness of owner-modified lower body wear.

Discrete Test: A test that nobody knows about.

Diagnostic Test: A test to determine specific strengths and weaknesses. (Attempting to use Skittles® in a math activity does not count.)

Formative Assessment: We devoted an entire chapter to this earlier. Weren't you paying attention? Drop and give me fifty!

Holistic Scoring: A method in which one overall score best represents the examinee's performance. Also known as a crock.[1]

High Stakes Testing: Here come those cannabis-eating cows again!

Indirect Testing: A generalized assessment that hits everything except the target you're actually aiming for. Much like bullets from bad guys in adventure movies.

---

[1] *A Swedish phrase that means "Yeah, right!"*

Integrated Test: A test that addresses multiple language skills, often in multiple languages. Capisce?

Multiple Choice Test: A type of assessment in which the student demonstrates his/her knowledge by selecting one response from a list of possible answers. Also known as guessing.

Needs Assessment: A formal inquiry into the current state of essential resources with the goal of taking specific action (usually extensive coffee drinking).

Off the Shelf: Commercially-available tests [1] which can be purchased by an educational institution and used at their discretion. Also refers to the clothing most teachers wear due to personal budget constraints (although the words "thrift shop" may also apply).

Performance Assessment: Often misused, this term originally meant a test that required the student to actively demonstrate a developed skill. Giving a speech, performing a skit, or painting a classmate are common examples.

Placement Test: An assessment whose results are used to assign students to groups designed to meet the needs of learners functioning at a certain level. Used to justify subtle forms of discrimination. (Okay … yes, I was in the "blackbird" group when I was a kid, and I've never gotten over it. So what, you snotty bluebirds?!)

---

[1] *Designed by "experts" who've never met an actual child*

Scale Score: A formal score that allows test results to be compared between students, reptiles, and fish.

Self-Assessment: A personal rating of a student's language arts, math, or science ability according to specified criteria. Also known as lying.

Stakeholders: Any persons involved with or invested in the testing process ... although when test scores are low, certain references to Bella Lagosi come to mind.

True/False Test: Similar to the Multiple-Choice Test except the odds are better.

Summative Assessment: This is the big daddy ... the end-of-the-year finale used in many states to rate schools, berate principals and teachers, and further politicians' careers.

Hopefully this list will lead you on your way towards a better understanding of testing terminology ... or at least towards buying a bigger coffee-maker.

"Tools make us more efficient.
Strategies make us more effective.
Habits make us more consistent."

Chapter 15: On a Serious Note

Throughout this book, we've poked fun at a number of sacred cows[1] in an attempt to make you smile. In this chapter, we'll review some serious resources that might make your life as a new teacher a bit easier. These are just my personal recommendations, but they're based on decades in the field[2] of education.

CLASSROOM MANAGEMENT

Harry Wong has probably done more than anyone on the planet to save the sanity of beginning teachers. ***The First Days of School: How to be an Effective Teacher*** has sold over three million copies, and many consider it the preeminent book on classroom management. Now in its fifth edition (anything around that long has stood the test of time), it's a "must read" for newbies.

If you don't already have one, get one. You can easily find it online or in most major book stores. More importantly, **read** it and follow the instructions! Like the plethora of exercise equipment and diet books that fill our homes, it only works if you actually *use* it.

---

[1] *Well, actually an entire herd*

[2] *Not the "business" of education. Public education is NOT a business and trying to draw parallels with the business world creates a very dangerous paradigm. But that's a different book.*

EFFECTIVE TEACHING

Mike Schmoker's ***Focus: Elevating the Essentials to Radically Improve Student Learning*** is a good place to start. I don't agree with everything in this book (for example, differentiated instruction can be a powerful tool when properly applied), but the overall message of "simplify, simplify, simplify" and his emphasis on solid, basic teaching is a welcome departure from the current trend of jumping from one new trend to another.[1]

Schmoker claims that effective, engaging lessons share the following characteristics:

- a clear learning objective
- an anticipatory set (tell 'em what you'll teach 'em)
- teaching in single, brief chunks (3 to 5 minutes)
- guided practice after each chunk (active interaction)
- multiple checks for understanding (vital!)
- adjust and reteach (as needed)
- independent practice, then final assessment

All of those are things we've known for years, but seem to have forgotten in the rush to implement the "next great thing." This progression also reflects the Gradual Release Model, which is all about getting students to take responsibility for their own learning and preparing them for the real world.

[1] *Often depending on what model the state is currently pushing or which conference the Superintendent recently attended*

TEACHING STRATEGIES

You've probably been exposed to dozens of teaching strategies in your training. Some will work better than others. Some work with one class, but not the next.

But like the gadgets in a mechanic's toolbox, mastery comes from having a broad selection to chose from and knowing which tool best fits the situation.[1]

Despite the humorous scenarios discussed in Chapter 5, I've personally found the following strategies to be very effective in my classrooms[2] ...

- think-pair-share
- cooperative learning
- inquiry-based instruction
- graphic organizers
- differentiated instruction
- learning stations (especially in K-4)
- four corners

There are multiple sources that describe each of these strategies in detail. But don't try to learn (or use) them all at once! Pick a strategy, try it out, and learn from the experience. Active interaction with students is almost always your best teacher.

[1] *Yes, a persistent person CAN remove a lugnut with a hammer and screwdriver, but a wrench is much more efficient.*
[2] *Caution: Like any tool, strategies are dangerous if misused.*

LESSON PLANNING

Good lesson planning is essential to good teaching. Unfortunately, in many cases it's become simply an act of compliance. Teachers rush to get something down on paper before the weekly deadline; principals simply glance at the submisisons to make sure they are done. Such a process does *nothing* to enhance student learning. In addition, years of focusing on high-stakes testing have led to "lesson plans" that are essentially just expanded lists of standards to be addressed.

By contrast, effective lesson plans are **learning** plans focused on student engagement. It's important to note that "Memorizing facts is boring. Drill and practice is boring. But for most students most of the time, *thinking* is actually fun!" [1]

The problem, of course, is that we've spent years training students to parrot back answers ... so the transition to getting them to function at a deeper level (reasoning, conjecturing, planning, analyzing, designing) can take some time. And it's critical that we learn to evaluate the success of our learning plans not by "did I cover the material?" or "did I address all the standards?" but by "What did the students actually learn?"

Once you understand what is and is not a good lesson plan, there are some great online sources for ideas. These include the Literacy Design Collaborative (multiple

---

[1] *Brookhart, S. (2016). Start with Higher-Order Thinking. Educational Leadership, (Vol. 74, Num. 2). ASCD.*

subject areas), the Mathematics Design Collaborative, Common Sense Education, and LinkedIn Learning (formerly Lynda.com). There are many more. Best of all, most of these are completely FREE.

PROFESSIONAL LEARNING COMMUNITIES

PLCs are based on an age-old concept: The better we communicate with one another, the more we understand. Great PLCs, whether online or on campus, are an ongoing process that start with three big ideas:

1) A focus on learning
2) A collaborative culture (collective responsibility)
3) An orientation on results

And whether it's a district-level team, a building-level team, or a content-based team, members of the PLC should always be working collaboratively to answer these four essential questions:

1) What do we want our students to learn?
2) How will we know if each student learns it?
3) How will we respond when some students have not learned it?
4) How can we extend learning for students who already know it?

To be truly effective, every PLC meeting must be have a clear goal, and at least one of these four essential questions must be addressed each time. And obviously, they must occur regularly.

Reflecting on and implementing the points above can help you become a much more effective PLC member.

And while the PLC process has been heavily commercialized in some states (occasionally leading to reasonable skepticism), properly implemented, it still remains an excellent tool for helping schools maintain a sustained focus on student learning.

ASSESSMENT

It's important to remember that the primary purpose of assessment is to monitor student progress so you can adjust classroom instruction. As Tim Shanahan points out, that means our primary focus should always be on the *teaching*, not the testing.[1]

Measurable student growth is our goal. And growth is always the result of effective teaching, not testing. Even the best testing is just a tool to let us know whether or not our teaching has been effective.

I realize that you may be in a state or district where excessive assessment is the norm. And it may be several more years before your legislators' addiction to high-stakes testing abates, so the temptation to "teach to the test" is strong. Do what you have to do to comply, but never lose sight of that fact that your real job is to help students learn to love *learning* ... not to love tests.

[1] *Shanahan, T. (2017). Let's Teach, Not Test. Retrieved from https:// shanahanonliteracy.com/blog/welcome-2017-lets-teach-not-test*

TECHNOLOGY

I remember when fax machines first came out.[1] There was a lot of hype about how this new technology would save hours and hours of time. Instead, office workers started using them to fax out for lunch.

New technology will always run the risk of unintended consequences, and there will always be students who will misuse whatever is available.[2] So how should we respond to this challenge?

On one extreme, we can ban technology from the classroom entirely, thus denying students the benefits that digital tools can provide. But there is a wealth of information and images that can be accessed by your students via tablets and computers, and interactive exploration can be a powerful learning tool.

On the other hand, we can allow an "open classroom" approach to technology, where students not only use school-supplied devices, but can also BYOT (bring your own tech). However, this opens the door to students wasting time playing games and hanging out on social media. And in such an "open" setting, that temptation is almost too much for the average child to bear.

Note that there are strong proponents for both of these approaches. The first group (Bauerlein, 2009; Goodwin,

---

[1] *Yes, unfortunately I'm really that old!*
[2] *Just like there were once boys who dunked the girls' pigtails in the inkwells.*

2015; Stoltfus, 2017; etc.) claim that "digital natives" are actually *less* literate than students of the past. The second group points out that technology is ubiquitous, and so to be successful, students need to master self-monitoring skills while they're still in school.

This argument is like most things in life ... the best course lies somewhere in the middle. And that often starts by developing a structured program with clear expectations.

This will not only help you maintain your focus on instruction, but will also make it much easier for you to deal with occasional breaches, since everyone knows what is expected up front.

A WORD ABOUT "RESEARCH"

In an age when "fake news" is applied to anything that anyone disagrees with (regardless of its validity), it's absolutely vital that both we and our students understand how to identify and apply reputable, credible sources of information.

Bogus or flawed research studies are not the only problem. A longitudinal study[1] from John Hopkins University found that "insider research" (studies sponsored by companies or special interest groups) show up to seventy percent more benefits than independent research!

[1] *Wolf, R., Morrison, J., Slavin, R., & Risman, K. (2019). Do Developer Commissioned Evaluations Inflate Impact Sizes?*

This emphasizes the importance of helping our students understand how due diligence when evaluating any source they use is vital. And this can start as early as the elementary grades through exposure to the basic logical fallacies that are designed to manipulate us.

For those who go on to college, it will help them avoid the embarrassment of quoting a questionable source. For those who don't, it will make them better consumers of news and information, and less likely to be manipulated by biased media and social media memes.

CONCLUSION

As mentioned earlier, these resources are just some of my personal favorites. There are many, many more. (We explore a lot of those in the grad courses I teach.)

But the most important thing to remember is that **our primary focus must always be on helping students learn**! Everything else is just tools and planning.

I hope you've enjoyed this book, and that in addition to some laughs, you've picked up a few useful tidbits along the way.

May your teaching career be packed with those "ah ha!" moments, and the deep, abiding joy of making a real, meaningful difference in student's lives.

> "When students are overwhelmed by strong emotions, it's usually advisable not to join them."[1]

---

[1] *Footnotes and sidebars throughout this book are a stylistic device that I first saw used in the works of the late Sir Terry Pratchett ... an English humorist, satirist, and author of fantasy novels (most notably the Discworld series). Their use throughout this book is my personal homage to this ultimate grandmaster of "the laughter that leads to introspection."*

Index

A
Alabama	p. 65
Anticipatory Sets	p. 24
Art Stations	p. 38

B
Biliousness	p. 57
Bracey, Gerald	p. 99
Bryun	pgs. 29, 33, 110
Brookhart, Susan	p. 118

C
Canabis-Consuming Cows	p. 96
Checks for Understanding (CFUs)	p. 27
Classroom Management	pgs. 7-9, **115**
Common Core Standards	pgs. 41-42
Communication Stations (reading/writing/listening)	p. 37
Concept Mapping	p. 33
Cooperative Learning	p. 32
Custom Curricula	pgs. 45-46
Curriculum Mapping	p. 49

D
Daily Lesson Plans	p. 55
Data (Star Trek)	pgs. 86, 106
Data Teams	p. 86
Direct Instruction	p. 31

E
Effective Environment	pgs. 11-13
Effective Teaching	pgs. 23-29, **116**
Essential Questions	p. 51
Extension Projects	p. 94

F
Failing Schools Myth	p. 101
Farticus	p. 52
Flavian Amphitheatre	p. 95
Formative Assessment	pgs. 89-95
Four Essential Questions	p. 75

G
Gradual Release Model	p. 29
Guided Practice	p. 26

H
Harry Wong	pgs. 5, x x
Hawaii	p. 41
High Stakes Testing	pgs. 97-105, **120**
Helmuth van Moltke	p. 51

I

Idaho	p. 65
Independent Learning	p. 34
Independent Practice	p. 29
Inquiry-Based Instruction	p. 35
Instructional Units	p. 47
Intervention Teams	p. 87

L

Learning Objectives	p. 23
Learning Stations	p. 37
Lederhosen	p. 60
Lesson Planning	pgs. 51-59, **118**

M

Math Stations	p. 38
Monitor & Adjust	p. 28
Multi-Tiered Support Systems	p. 83

N

Nebraska	p. 58
New York	p. 8
Non-Linguistic Representations	p. 39

O

Oklahoma	p. 5
One Minute Papers	p. 90

P

Pole Dancers	p. 90
Professional Learning Communities (PLCs)	pgs. 71-81, **119**
Progress Monitoring	p. 86

R

Red Hot Chili Peppers	p. 82
Response to Intervention (RTI)	pgs. 83-87
Round Robin Charts	p. 92

S

Scaffolding	p. 32
School Culture	pgs. 61-73
Science Stations	p. 37
Shanahan, Tim	p. 120
State Curriculum Standards	pgs. 41-43

T

Teaching Strategies	pgs. 31-39, **117**
Tests (criterion vs norm)	pgs. 107-108
Testing Terminology	pgs. 108-110
Texas	p. 41
TIMSS Test	pgs. 101-102
Toxic vs. Positive Culture	p. 61
Twitter Summaries	p. 9

W

Wind-Driven, Pitch Approximator	p. 63
Wolf, Morrison, Slavin, Risman	p. 122

Since opportunities for giving offense are quite numerous in a loose work of satire like this, "Justin Case" is obviously a pseudonym created to protect the guilty.

The real author of this book is passionate about teaching and learning. Among other things, he (or is it she?) was a finalist for state **Teacher of the Year**, has served as both an elementary and high school principal, worked as a consultant on several elementary curricula, has authored several books (serious ones), and today teaches graduate courses for a major university.

More importantly, (s)he has a deep conviction that every aspect of education should not only be meaningful, but also **FUN** ... and that concept applies to both learning *and* teaching!

Neuro-scientists tell us **it is literally impossible** to think deeply about something you really don't care about. Thus engaging your students (and yourself) in active, enjoyable learning lies at the very heart of all effective instruction.

So if this book not only made you chuckle, but also made you think a bit more deeply, then it has served its purpose.

"Education is not filling a bucket, it's lighting a fire!"[1]

– W.B. Yeats

[1] *Yanking the fire alarm is optional.*

You have now reached the end of this book.

I hope you enjoyed reading it as much as I enjoyed writing it.

Now put it down and go outdoors!

In case you've forgotten by now, the real ones are in color!

Made in the USA
Columbia, SC
20 August 2021